Headline Series   S0-AEG-771

No. 288   **FOREIGN POLICY ASSOCIATION**   Spring 1989

IN OUR IMAGE

America's Empire in the Philippines

by Stanley Karnow

Cover Design: Ed Bohon $4.00

The Author

STANLEY KARNOW began his journalistic career in Paris in 1950 as a *Time* correspondent. After covering Europe, Africa and the Middle East, he went to Asia for *Time* and *Life* in 1959, and subsequently reported from there for the London *Observer, The Saturday Evening Post, The Washington Post* and NBC News. He was an editor of *The New Republic* and a columnist for King Features. His books include *Southeast Asia; Mao and China: From Revolution to Revolution;* and *Vietnam: A History,* on which HEADLINE SERIES No. 263, "Vietnam: The War Nobody Won," is based. He won six Emmys as chief correspondent for *Vietnam: A Television History,* and is the recipient of two Overseas Press Club Awards for newspaper reporting.

© Catherine Karnow

Born in New York City, Mr. Karnow graduated from Harvard and attended the Ecole des Sciences Politiques in Paris. He has been a Nieman Fellow, Kennedy Fellow and East Asia Research Center Fellow at Harvard, and Poynter Fellow at Yale. Married to Annette Karnow, a painter, he has three children and lives in Potomac, Maryland.

The Foreign Policy Association

The Foreign Policy Association is a private, nonprofit, nonpartisan educational organization. Its purpose is to stimulate wider interest and more effective participation in, and greater understanding of, world affairs among American citizens. Among its activities is the continuous publication, dating from 1935, of the HEADLINE SERIES. The author is responsible for factual accuracy and for the views expressed. FPA itself takes no position on issues of U.S. foreign policy.

HEADLINE SERIES (ISSN 0017-8780) is published four times a year, Winter, Spring, Summer and Fall, by the Foreign Policy Association, Inc., 729 Seventh Ave., New York, N.Y. 10019. Chairman, Robert V. Lindsay; President, John W. Kiermaier; Editor in Chief, Nancy L. Hoepli; Senior Editors, Ann R. Monjo and K.M. Rohan. Subscription rates, $15.00 for 4 issues; $25.00 for 8 issues; $30.00 for 12 issues. Single copy price $4.00. Discount 25% on 10 to 99 copies; 30% on 100 to 499; 35% on 500 to 999; 40% on 1,000 or more. Payment must accompany all orders. Add $1.75 for postage. USPS #238-340. Second-class postage paid at New York, N.Y. POSTMASTER: Send address changes to HEADLINE SERIES, Foreign Policy Association, 729 Seventh Ave., New York, N.Y. 10019. Copyright 1989 by Foreign Policy Association, Inc. Composed and printed at Science Press, Ephrata, Pennsylvania. Spring 1989.

Library of Congress Catalog Card No. 89-80555
ISBN 0-87124-124-2

1

All in the Family

By September 1986, after four years as secretary of state, George P. Shultz had grown accustomed to presiding over official dinners for foreign dignitaries visiting Washington: the rigorous protocol, the solemn oratory, the contrived cordiality. But he could not recall an occasion equal to this night. He was honoring Corazon Cojuangco Aquino, the new president of the Philippines, and a spontaneous charge of emotion electrified the affair. Americans and Filipinos had shared history, tragedy, triumph, ideals—experiences that had left them with a sense of kinship. Shultz captured that spirit exactly: A "Cory" doll pinned to his lapel, his Buddha-like face beamed and his nasal voice lilted with rare elation. Breaking with routine, he delivered his toast before the banquet—in effect telling the guests to relax and enjoy. "This," he said, "is a family evening."

Cory's appeal transcended her American connections. Seven

From the book *In Our Image: America's Empire in the Philippines* by Stanley Karnow. Copyright © 1989 by Stanley Karnow. Reprinted with the permission of Random House, Inc.

Robert Mansfield

CHINA

HONG KONG

TAIWAN

HAINAN

VIETNAM

LAOS

CAMBODIA

South China Sea

Philippine Sea

LUZON

Manila

PHILIPPINES

MINDORO

PANAY

SAMAR

NEGROS

MINDANAO

PALAWAN

BRUNEI

MALAYSIA

SINGAPORE

INDONESIA

Miles

0   400

Clark Air Base

Angeles

Subic Naval Base

Subic

Manila

Corregidor

months earlier, she had toppled Ferdinand E. Marcos in an episode almost too melodramatic to be true—a morality play, a reenactment of the Passion: The pious widow of Marcos's chief opponent, the martyred Benigno "Ninoy" Aquino Jr., she had risen from his death to rally her people against the corrupt despot, his egregious wife and their wicked regime. Throughout the world she became an instant celebrity, a household icon: the saintly Cory who, perhaps through divine intervention, had emerged from obscurity to exorcise evil. Elsewhere in Asia, in Taiwan and in South Korea, demonstrators invoked her name in their protests against autocracy.

Most Americans may have forgotten, perhaps never even knew, that the Philippines had been a U.S. possession; for those who remembered, Cory symbolized anew that special relationship. During its half century of colonial tutelage, America had endowed the Filipinos with universal education, a common language, public hygiene, roads, bridges and, above all, republican institutions. Americans and Filipinos had fought and died side by side at Bataan and Corregidor and perished together on the ghastly Death March. The United States was still in the Philippines, the site of its two largest overseas bases, and more than a million Filipinos lived in America. By backing Marcos, even as an expedient, the United States had betrayed its protégés and its own principles, but, as if by miracle, Cory Aquino had redeemed her nation—and redeemed America as well.

Shultz's role in her achievement, though belated, had been decisive. He was frustrated by unresolved challenges: Central America, the Middle East, negotiations with the Soviet Union. Not the least of his problems were his rivals in President Ronald Reagan's entourage, constantly nibbling at his authority. Here he had scored a visible victory: He had finally won the Washington debate over dumping Marcos—despite recollections of the disasters that had followed past U.S. maneuvers against such unwanted clients as South Vietnamese President Ngo Dinh Diem and the shah of Iran. At his urgent behest, Reagan begrudgingly consented to discard Marcos and hustle him off to Honolulu. A bloodbath had been narrowly averted in Manila, and Cory had restored democracy to the Philippines. Now, on this autumn evening, Cory beside him, Shultz savored her success, his success. In what for him was an explosion of enthusiasm, he remarked that the occasion had "a real good feel to it."

Even the chronically foul Washington weather felt good. The summer heat had faded, leaving the air as soft as satin. From the terrace outside the State Department's top-floor dining room, the capital resembled a tourist poster. Lights flooded the Washington Monument and the majestic dome of the Capitol and between them, like a giant lantern, hung a full harvest moon as yellow as butter. Aquino, while enduring her husband's imprisonment under Marcos, had borrowed yellow as her signature color from the poignant Civil War ballad: "Tie a Yellow Ribbon Around the Old Oak Tree." When a guest noted the felicitous coincidence, Shultz's spokesman, Bernard Kalb, quipped, "The Central Intelligence Agency (CIA) can do anything."

Cory desperately needed economic aid and investment, and Shultz had carefully reviewed the guest list, inviting a heavy-weight contingent from Congress along with some of America's major bankers and corporate executives. Present, too, were the handful of State Department officials who had lobbied for her against Reagan's reticence and the opposition of his staff. Diplomats, publishers, journalists, scholars and lawyers were also there, and a group of influential Filipino businessmen had flown in from Manila. The place was "loaded," Shultz said proudly, with "important people who make things happen."

Old Grievances, Old Loyalties

Vice President George Bush, acting as official greeter, had paid a call on Aquino the previous day at her hotel suite. As they posed for the photo opportunity, she smiled stiffly. Of course she would not spoil the occasion by dredging up old grievances, but Bush was anathema to her for his effulgent praise of Marcos during a visit to Manila in 1981. The Marcoses, masters at lavishing attention on important guests, had laid on an opulent dinner for him at the Malacañang, the presidential palace. Scripted by the State Department to reassure Marcos of the Reagan Administration's "friendship," Bush toasted Marcos's "adherence to democratic principles and to the democratic processes." The inane remark had clung to him for years, and he knew that Cory remembered it. Now, however, he sought to reassure her. There was "no resistance of any kind to you" within the Administration, he told her, predicting that she and Reagan would "get along very well . . . in terms of chemistry."

He was wrong. A man who prized loyalty, Reagan stuck by those who had been faithful to him—a trait he displayed in his reluctance to dismiss unethical subordinates. Nor did he easily shed illusions, as in his tendency to confuse movies with reality. Whatever Marcos's faults, he still esteemed him an "old friend and ally," an intrepid anti-Japanese guerrilla during World War II and a veteran "freedom fighter" in the struggle against communism. Besides, he had never forgotten his first trip to Manila in 1969, when he was governor of California. President Richard M. Nixon had sent him and Nancy there to represent the United States at the opening of a cultural center, and the Marcoses had treated them like royalty. By contrast, he instinctively distrusted Cory.

Reagan's Rebuff

Not until April, a full two months after her victory, did he personally congratulate her by telephone. She interpreted the delay as an indirect reproach—and, a few days later, he exacerbated it with a gesture that she could justifiably consider an insult. En route to Asia, he had stopped for a few days in Hawaii and actually contemplated driving over to see Marcos, who was now living there in splendid exile. Shultz had all he could do to dissuade him, and Reagan telephoned Marcos instead. Marcos, his voice slurred, carried on almost endlessly, insisting that he was still the rightful president of the Philippines, denouncing Cory as incompetent and soft on communism and complaining about his confiscated property. His wife, Imelda, pouring out her heart to Nancy, blubbered that the press had maligned her with exaggerated reports of the thousands of shoes and sundry glitz she had left behind in Manila. The maudlin performance embarrassed the

Reagans—all the more so because Imelda, to show that the Marcos connection with the United States was intact, had violated the privacy of the conversation by arranging for a Honolulu television station to broadcast a silent segment. Administration spokesmen, fearing that Reagan's contact with Marcos might alarm Cory, hastily expressed his endorsement of her, but she was unconvinced. She continued to believe that Reagan still yearned for Marcos's restoration to power. And now, five months afterward, as her motorcade sped to the White House, she was rankled as well by Reagan's refusal to elevate her journey to Washington to the full panoply of a "state visit"—an honor that he had accorded the Marcoses in September 1982, which in diplomatic semiotics signified unqualified recognition as a chief of state.

Her intuition was not misplaced. Though Reagan had by now reconciled himself to her ascension to office, he still harbored misgivings about her abilities. But he was a courtly host. After an amiable luncheon with Cory, he listened to her account of the "economic devastation" caused by Marcos's excesses. He was "bullish" on the Philippines, he said, and vowed to "do all we can" to help in its recovery. His real concern, however, was the Communist insurrection nagging the country. Aquino, who had recently begun discussions with the rebels under a cease-fire, explained to him that she was seeking a political solution while keeping open her "military option." The strategy struck him as naïve, even dangerous. After all, he was dedicated to the effort of the contras to topple the left-wing Sandinista regime in Nicaragua and, he implied, she had to act tough. Emphasizing the importance of force, he cautioned her to watch herself. "I've had experience dealing with Communists," he said.

Cory Conquers Congress's Heart

But the climax of her Washington visit, Cory realized, would be her appearance before a joint session of Congress—where the money was. The address, designed to appeal to liberals and conservatives alike, omitted mention of America's bases in the Philippines—a divisive issue among Filipinos and one Cory preferred to shelve for the time being. She added a passage about her assassinated husband. The words, however, were less dynamic than the picture she would portray of herself. As Cory, the plucky little housewife who had crushed the malevolent Marcos, her conquest of Capitol Hill was virtually guaranteed.

She spoke earnestly and confidently for half an hour, pausing only for the dozen bursts of applause—her eloquent English a further reminder to the assembly, if it were necessary, that she was the product of America's tutelage of the Philippines, educated in American schools.

Their "three happiest years" had been her family's exile in Boston. Out of honest gratitude she said, "Thank you, America, for the haven from oppression." Then, striking a sincerely religious chord, she invoked the "brazen" murder of her husband in Manila in August 1983, presumably at Marcos's doing, intoning: "His death was my country's resurrection." Filipinos "threw aside their passivity and fear" to propel her drive against Marcos. "And so began the revolution that has brought me to democracy's most famous home, the Congress of the United States."

But now an insurrection that thrived on poverty and injustice threatened democracy in the Philippines. Her goal, Cory said, was to lure the Communist rebels out of the hills, and win them over "by economic progress and justice . . . for which the best intentioned among them fight." Only by exploring "the path of peace" would she have "the moral basis" for "picking up the sword of war" if her effort faltered. She believed in Lincoln's dictum—"with malice toward none, with charity for all." Like him, she understood that "force may be necessary before mercy."

In any case, American aid was indispensable. Marcos's profligate rule had left the Philippines with a foreign debt of $26 billion; the interest alone cost half its annual export earnings. Congress failed to ease the burden—even though, Cory chided, "ours must have been the cheapest revolution ever." Nevertheless, Filipinos had backed her campaign to clamor for democracy, however abstract the concept may have been to them. "Slum or impoverished village," she said, "they came to me with one cry: Democracy! Not food, though they clearly needed it, not work, though they surely wanted it—but democracy." So her question for Congress—and for America—was plain: "Has there been a greater test of national commitment to the ideals you hold dear than what my people have gone through? You have spent many lives and much treasure to bring freedom to many lands that were reluctant to receive it. And here you have a people who won it by themselves and need only help to preserve it."

A volcanic ovation erupted. Engulfing Cory as she descended from the podium, legislators cheered, applauded and jostled one another as they reached to grasp her hand. "That was the finest speech I've heard in my 34 years in Congress," exclaimed Thomas P. "Tip" O'Neill (D-Mass.), who from his perch as House speaker had been looking down with avuncular benevolence during her address. The chamber again chanted "Cory, Cory, Cory" as she walked up the aisle, escorted by Senator Robert Dole (Kans.), the leader of the Republican majority. "You hit a home run," he remarked to her—to which she snapped back without hesitation, "I hope the bases were loaded."

But if Cory had belted the ball, as Senator Dole had cracked, the game was being played on a soggy field. Within five hours of her speech, the House of Representatives increased aid to the Philippines by $200 million above the half-billion dollars already appropriated, but the measure passed by only six votes. "We voted with our hearts, not our heads," said one member regretfully, explaining that foreign aid was poison at this time of budgetary constraints. Ten days later, the Senate rejected the package. Dole was responsible for the rebuff despite his encomium for Cory. Her silence on the U.S. bases in the Philippines had vexed him, as it had several other Republican senators. He was also determined to prove that he would not be suckered by sentimentality. The House decision, he said sardonically, had given Cory "the biggest honorarium in history"; it was "not very good policy" that "because someone came here and made a speech, they get $200 million." Only through a "mushy compromise," as one congressman phrased it, were the extra funds subsequently approved.

President Corazon Aquino takes the oath of office at the Club Filipino in Manila on February 25, 1986.

Future aid proposals sparked fresh debates on Capitol Hill, leaving Filipinos wondering whether Cory's stirring performance in Washington would translate into consistent U.S. support. Even Secretary of State Shultz, his affection for the Philippines notwithstanding, put a limit on American help. Cory's vice-president, Salvador H. Laurel, once begged him for urgent economic assistance, saying, "Our needs are infinite." "That may be," Shultz replied, "but our resources are not."

Power and Survival

Revisiting Manila over the next few years, I found Cory to be increasingly comfortable with power. Despite her family fortune, she had never flaunted her wealth. Besides, she wanted to project an image of austerity after the outrageous ostentation of the Marcoses. She chose to live in a modest house rather than move into the Malacañang, the ornate presidential palace, studiously avoiding flamboyance of the kind that had become Imelda's trademark. But, no longer shy and self-effacing, she was not afraid to assert her authority over the veteran politicians to whom, as Ninoy's dutiful wife, she had once served coffee. She also seemed to be learning the difference between the poetry of revolution and the prose of government. Rallies and rhetoric, she realized, were not going to solve unemployment or defeat insurgents. Nor did she address every challenge by asking herself what Ninoy would do. "I reached the point," she told me, "when I knew that I was president, not Ninoy, and that I had to make the decisions."

After three years in office, though still popular, her reputation had eroded—largely because she could not have conceivably lived up to the image of miracle worker that her own supporters had originally pinned on her. The Marcos legacy was a daunting enough burden for her to bear. But she had inherited a sprawling archipelago of disparate languages and cultures that owed its semblance of unity mainly to the legal definition of Filipino citizenship and an allegiance to the Catholic Church. Despite its modern trappings, it was still a feudal society dominated by an oligarchy of rich dynasties, which had evolved from one of the world's longest continuous spans of Western imperial rule.

2

The American Legacy

First came Spain and then the United States—or, as the neat summation of Philippine history goes: "Three centuries in a Catholic convent and 50 years in Hollywood."

Ferdinand Magellan, a Portuguese explorer flying the flag of Spain, stumbled onto the islands in 1521 in his search for the lucrative spices of the Indies. He died there, a victim of his own imprudence, and his ships sailed on—one of them to complete the first circumnavigation of the globe. Other Spaniards returned and remained, even though the archipelago was not the El Dorado of their dreams. Manila was convenient for trade with nearby China, and the provinces offered the Catholic Church a fertile field for saving souls. So, under Spain, the Philippines became the only Christian country of Asia—and, through Christianity, the West's first foothold in the region. Spain left another heritage, in the form of land grants to Spanish settlers—which, passed on to rich Filipino *mestizo* families, created the oligarchy that wields power today. Coupled with her American education, Cory Aquino personifies the legacy of the Spanish era. Her intense piety stems from an almost medieval brand of Spanish Catholicism, and she owes her private fortune to a Chinese great-grandfather who acquired large properties a century ago.

Spain, itself in a cocoon, sealed off the Philippines from the outside world until the nineteenth century, when liberal Spanish kings opened the islands to foreign trade. The landed gentry prospered from the global demand for sugar and other commodities stimulated by the industrial revolution. Seeking recognition to match their wealth, they began to defy their imperial Spanish masters long before the elite of other European possessions in Asia challenged their rulers. The Filipino clergy agitated for equality with Spanish priests. Affluent young Filipinos, sent by their fathers to study in Europe, returned home from the heady atmosphere of Madrid, Paris and Berlin with enlightened ideas that, to the Spanish administration in Manila, seemed subversive.

The most brilliant of them, José Rizal y Mercado, oculist, poet, painter and writer, fueled the ferment with his polemical novels. Cautious and conservative, he championed integration with Spain rather than independence. But reactionary Spanish priests and officials in Manila, resistant to even the mildest change, railroaded him to execution in 1896. Filipinos, for whom the Passion is a reality, perceived in his martyrdom an imitation of Christ's agony, and they have revered him since as a quasireligious national hero—a status they have also begun to confer on Ninoy Aquino.

Rizal's death ignited a rebellion against Spain led by Emilio Aguinaldo y Famy, a dashing if naïve young Filipino whose objective was independence. Most Americans had never heard of the Philippines, but they were soon to become embroiled in the conflict as the United States reached across the Pacific for the first time in its history.

America was then going through a stupendous transition as dynamic entrepreneurs and a restive immigrant population transformed its vast resources into an industrial powerhouse. But Americans were split over the issue of whether to project their new power overseas or to concentrate their energies at home. With nuanced differences, essentially the same debate over global priorities has preoccupied the nation since.

'Manifest Destiny'

The imperialists, advocates of a strong American presence abroad, included figures like the young assistant secretary of the Navy Theodore Roosevelt, Senator Henry Cabot Lodge (R-Mass.) and Captain Alfred Mahan, the scholarly naval strategist. Only as a world power, they affirmed, could the United States trade, prosper and protect itself against its potential enemies. This role, they maintained, was America's manifest destiny—a phrase originally coined to promote the settlement of the West. William Randolph Hearst, lord of the yellow press, was their publicist. Though mostly Republicans, they were backed by the Populists, poor farmers of the Middle West who blamed their economic problems on foreign bankers, and so thrilled to the idea of fighting any foreigners. They had no plans at that stage to grab territory, as the Europeans were doing in Asia and Africa. Their vague objective was to make America a voice on the international scene. For Teddy Roosevelt, war itself was the highest form of human endeavor.

Various motives inspired the anti-imperialists. Tycoons like Andrew Carnegie asserted that costly foreign ventures would divert America from the development of its domestic economy. An older generation of Americans, recalling the horrors of the Civil War, flinched at the thought of another conflict. The northern factory workers and southern farmers who supported the Democratic party tended to be isolationist. Grover Cleveland, the former president and a Democrat, delayed the annexation of Hawaii as long as he could, and William Jennings Bryan, the party standard-bearer, was equivocal on the issue.

The imperialists prevailed in 1898. The United States went to war with Spain—the first war waged by America beyond its continental boundaries. An inexorable force drove the nation into war, but like all wars, it was not inevitable.

It began over Cuba, where rebels were struggling against Spanish tyranny. Skilled Cuban propagandists in the United States, abetted by Hearst and other sensationalists, had won America's sympathy. American investors in Cuba favored an end to Spanish rule. For the Spanish, whose Latin American empire had crumbled, Cuba was a last vestige of past grandeur—and its potential loss had already ignited political passions in Spain. The queen, traumatized by the threat to her tottering throne, had nevertheless edged toward compromise, and a strong U.S. President might have given her time. But, though the prospect of war alarmed him, William McKinley was weak and indecisive. He waffled for nearly two months following the mysterious sinking of the *Maine* in Havana harbor on February 15, 1898, while hawks whipped up the fervor. Finally, still befuddled, he allowed Congress to push him into a conflict he neither wanted nor understood. Least of all did he grasp the purpose of the offensive against the Philippines.

The Conquest of the Philippines

Congress had affirmed at the outset that America intended to free, not acquire, Cuba. But America's ultimate goal for the Philippines, a sideshow to the main Cuban arena, was left undefined. There, on secret orders from Roosevelt, a U.S. fleet commanded by Commodore George Dewey had sunk a decrepit Spanish armada in Manila Bay in a few hours on the morning of May 1, 1898. McKinley pondered the problem of what to do with the archipelago—which he could not find on the map.

He complied with Dewey's request for forces to secure his victory, and in another historical first, U.S. troops crossed the Pacific. They occupied Manila shortly afterward under an arrangement with the Spanish while McKinley continued to contemplate the future of the Philippines. Eventually, he later revealed to a group of clergymen, God told him to annex the islands and "do the best we could for them."

Unlike Presidents today, McKinley rarely committed himself to paper, and the scant record contains no clues to the thinking that went into his decision. So historians have conjectured that, given his malleable character, he was carried along by a momentum that he either would not or could not control—just as he had been propelled into the war with Spain.

Even ardent imperialists initially spurned the notion of retaining the Philippines. At most, they reckoned, the United States might keep a naval base or trading station in Manila. But the dream of empire gradually germinated in the minds of Americans. Some envisioned the archipelago as the pivot of a booming commerce with China. Christian missionaries hoped to convert pagans, and ideologues saw America as the master of "inferior races." Strategists warned that another foreign power—most likely Japan or Germany—would grab the islands if the United States withdrew. Rudyard Kipling, the literary apostle of British imperialism, also exerted influence. He deliberately wrote his famous poem "The White Man's Burden" as an exhortation to Americans to bestow the blessings of their civilization on the Philippines—though, he warned, it would be a thankless task.

The acquisition of the archipelago appalled New York and Boston patricians, many of them old abolitionists who equated the subjugation of people overseas with slavery. Their objections were echoed by such eminent figures as Mark Twain, then at the peak of his fame, and the philosopher William James. Distinguished jurists cautioned that colonialism breached the constitutional principle of "government by consent of the governed." But not all the anti-imperialists were high-minded moralists. Bigots among them feared that America, by assuming responsibilities in Asia, would be contaminated by "Mongoloid barbarians."

The Forgotten War

The Senate debate over annexation of the Philippines in early 1899 was both eloquent and bitter—and symptomatic of the nation's schism over the issue of imperialism. Meanwhile, tensions gripped Manila as U.S. troops blocked the Filipino nationalist forces from entering the city. On the night of February 4, a Nebraska volunteer named Willie Grayson shot a Filipino soldier, and fighting broke out. Two days later, the Senate narrowly voted to keep the islands. But a new war had erupted between the United States and Aguinaldo's army. It is one of the forgotten wars of American history.

Though he had declared independence, Aguinaldo would probably have been amenable to an arrangement that granted autonomy to the Philippines under an American protectorate. But the U.S. commanders on the spot, Dewey and Major General Elwell Otis, were fatuous and arrogant men with neither the inclination nor the sensitivity to explore Filipino aspirations. Nor was McKinley, who by now had opted for annexation, in a mood to consider concessions. American history books refer to the war that followed as the "insurrection," as if the Filipinos were rebelling against legitimate U.S. authority. In reality it was an unalloyed American conquest of territory and among the cruelest conflicts in the annals of Western imperialism. At its peak, 70,000 U.S. soldiers were involved, and by its end in 1901, at least 200,000 Filipino civilians had been killed.

Aguinaldo blundered from the start by engaging America's superior forces in large battles. Realizing his mistake, he soon switched to guerrilla tactics, but as a conservative nationalist rather than a social reformer, he failed to promote the changes necessary to win his partisans the support of the peasantry. Isolated, his ranks enfeebled by dissension and defections, he retreated to a remote village in northern Luzon. There he was captured in a bold maneuver by the swashbuckling Colonel Frederick Furston. The Americans pursued the remnant Filipino troops in brutal operations, one so severe that it led to the court-martial of a U.S. general, Jacob Smith.

After Victory, Torment

It was not a living-room war visible to Americans on television, as Vietnam would be two generations later. Unlike in Vietnam, the United States won. Yet there were similarities: Accounts of American atrocities, aired in the U.S. press and in Senate hearings, soured the public at home on the conflict—which in any case dragged on too long. What had started as a glorious mission became a torment. Americans lost their enthusiasm for foreign ventures—just as, in the aftermath of Vietnam, they shunned the role of global policeman. The United States continued to practice forms of economic and political imperialism in the years ahead, but territorial conquest began and ended in the Philippines.

Lacking a colonial vocation, the Americans experimented in the Philippines. Judged in retrospect, the performance was neither as brilliant as their publicists claimed nor as bleak as their critics contended. They never quite fulfilled their hope of transforming the Filipinos into facsimile Americans. But in contrast to the Europeans, they were uniquely benign, almost sentimental imperialists. As a result, Filipinos today feel a closer affinity for America than, say, Indians do for Britain or Vietnamese for France. The million or so Filipinos living in the United States are the largest Asian minority in terms of their country's population— and, given their high birthrate, they will be the biggest by the end of this century. Thousands of Filipinos have "green cards"— permits to reside in America. Nearly 300,000 Filipinos request authorization to visit the United States every year, and the waiting list for immigration visas is 42 years long. I once asked a Filipino on the long line at the American consulate in Manila why he wanted to go to the United States. Surprised by such an obvious question, he replied, "America is my other home."

Different economic impulses distinguished European from American imperialism. The British, French and Dutch, with their limited domestic economies, perceived colonial markets and sources of raw materials to be vital to their prosperity. British firms developed tin mines and rubber plantations in Malaya, employing coolie labor under horrendous conditions, and French companies in Vietnam owned rice estates the size of provinces. On the other hand, Americans saw their fortunes at home, in tapping seemingly limitless coal, oil and mineral deposits, building steel mills and railroads, manufacturing and selling consumer products to an immense population and financing all these projects. So Congress could afford to appear ethical—as it did by barring American individuals and corporations from acquiring large landholdings in the Philippines. Filipinos were thus spared exploitation of the kind practiced by the Europeans.

But they were not saved from a classical colonial trade bind. American business was given a virtual import monopoly in the Philippines, for which Filipinos received tariff-free access to the United States for their commodities. Though apparently reciprocal, the arrangement actually stunted the growth of Philippine industry and preserved the archipelago as an agricultural society reliant on the American market. It also perpetuated the power of the Filipino upper class, which derived its wealth from the land. The United States forced the same pattern on the Filipinos after independence, thereby making a mockery of their sovereignty.

Compared to the Europeans, the Americans were far more liberal politically. Though they restricted the vote to the educated class, they nevertheless encouraged elections soon after their arrival, so that the Filipinos had a national legislature, the first in Asia, as early as 1907. Nine years later, in an unprecedented gesture for an imperial power, they pledged eventual freedom for the Philippines. This was a time when the British, despite their own democratic creed, were detaining Indian dissidents without trial and the French, for all their dedication to the principles of liberty, equality and fraternity, were summarily executing Vietnamese nationalists.

But the Americans neglected to establish an effective and impartial administration in the Philippines—as the British did in the creation of the Indian Civil Service, still a model of efficiency. So Filipinos turned to politicians instead of the bureaucracy for assistance, a practice that fostered patronage and corruption. Nor were the Americans, with all their professions of righteousness, as racially tolerant as the French or the Dutch. Prior to World War II, an American who married a Filipino woman was banished from the American community in Manila.

In many ways, the Filipinos were easier to co-opt than other Asians. The Indians, Vietnamese and Indonesians had a sense of their national character. They could gaze with pride at stone temples that symbolized their past grandeur. Their myths told of victories over alien invaders, of distant divine emperors and legendary warriors whose spirits evoked their nationhood. Western imperialism had violated their ancient culture, and many resisted it by recalling their history. By contrast, the history of the Philippines was colonial history. The Filipinos lacked fabled kings and heroes; the saints they worshiped were Western rather than Filipino. Before Spain arrived, they had been an assortment of tribes, without a central authority, a single language or a common religion. Untrammeled by strong feelings of national exclusivity, they were more receptive than other Asians to foreign influence. Their elite, Westernized long before the upper classes in Europe's colonies, welcomed the United States as a salutary force for modernization, not as a threat to tradition. Numbers of educated Filipinos abandoned Aguinaldo's movement, preferring instead the benison of U.S. rule. Spain had brought them Christianity; now they awaited adoption by the Americans.

Secular missionaries, the Americans zealously went forth with the conviction that the United States was the greatest society ever created, and they hoped to infuse less-privileged peoples with their ideals. In the wake of the conquest of the Philippines, they did strive to accomplish that goal. "Benevolent assimilation," McKinley termed the concept, and his secretary of war, Elihu Root, refined it. The U.S. colonial administration, Root prescribed, must promote the "happiness, peace and prosperity" of the Filipinos, but its measures should "conform to their customs, their habits and even their prejudices." Underlying the policy was the theory that the Filipinos, converted by the virtues of their American masters, would submit to their own transformation. The policy proved to be remarkably effective—up to a point.

'Americanizing,' then 'Filipinizing' Colonial Rule

William Howard Taft, a corpulent Ohio judge, landed in Manila in June 1900 as the first U.S. civilian governor. He went on to become secretary of war and later President and, more than any other American, he shaped the contours of U.S. rule in the Philippines during its first decade.

Reflecting the racist attitudes of his time, he was not particularly fond of the Filipinos. But obedient to Root's instructions, he undertook to Americanize "our little brown brothers," as he condescendingly called them. He built ports and roads to unify the Philippines and develop its economy. To instill in Filipinos the fundamentals of democracy, he assigned young American teachers to schools throughout the archipelago. Finally, he launched a program of political tutelage to prepare the Filipinos to govern themselves, and helped them to found a political party, the *Federalistas,* whose platform advocated statehood for the

Philippines. The foundations Taft laid remained largely unshaken during the entire period of U.S. rule—and they have not been completely dismantled. A statehood party exists to this day.

The Taft era ended in 1913 with the inauguration of Woodrow Wilson, the first Democratic President in 16 years, who assigned Francis Burton Harrison as Manila's new governor. A progressive, Harrison purged the colonial bureaucracy of its Americans and supplanted them with Filipinos. The process, called Filipinization, effectively put the Filipinos in charge of their own affairs for the next three decades of American rule. In 1935, true to its promise, the United States granted the Philippines internal autonomy under a commonwealth government—with total independence scheduled for 10 years later.

But U.S. policies, though liberal by colonial standards, were flawed. American education endowed the Philippines for the first time in its history with a lingua franca, English, which discouraged the development of a national language. The United States introduced the Filipinos to democratic institutions without requiring them to respect the substance of democracy. On the contrary, Taft had vested authority in the *ilustrados,* the rich intelligentsia, whose conservative beliefs he shared, and his successors endorsed their power on the theory that the Filipinos deserved to govern themselves. The landowners and entrepreneurial classes naturally recoiled from economic and social reforms that would have curbed their prerogatives, preferring instead to preserve a feudal system—even though it perpetuated and even widened the shocking gap between wealth and poverty. American officials, long aware of these inequities, only began to suggest improvements in the 1930s, when President Franklin D. Roosevelt's New Deal made it stylish to recommend radical change. By then, however, it was too late. The Filipinos were virtually sovereign; besides, interference in their internal affairs would have smelled of wicked imperialism.

Filipinos, however, yearned for American patronage. Just as Spanish sponsorship had assured them wealth and prestige in the nineteenth century, so American endorsement was the key to success. The two most prominent Filipino political figures of the

U.S. colonial period, Sergio Osmeña and Manuel Luis Quezon y Molina, owed their careers to American mentors. As president of the commonwealth, Quezon entrusted the formation of a national Philippine army to General Douglas MacArthur, his ritual brother. Even the Philippine Communist party was founded under the auspices of clandestine American Communist comrades. American officers commanded Filipino troops during World War II, and the pattern persisted after independence. MacArthur, restoring the old oligarchy following the war, engineered the election of Manuel Roxas y Acuña as first president of the sovereign Philippine republic. The most popular postwar president, Ramon Magsaysay, was virtually invented by Colonel Edward Lansdale, a secret American operative. Marcos was delighted when President Lyndon B. Johnson called him "my right arm in Asia," and he reveled in being termed Reagan's "old friend." Aquino attributed her election in early 1986 to God and public revulsion against Marcos—an unbeatable alchemy. But Marcos, who also claimed victory, might not have stepped down without a shove from Washington.

Role of the CIA

Many Filipinos, assuming that every political event in the Philippines is due to U.S. intervention, credit Americans and especially the CIA with superhuman powers. They suspect American correspondents, businessmen and professors as well as Peace Corps volunteers of working for the CIA, and the suspicion is understandable. The CIA has in fact been a formidable influence over the years. Aside from Magsaysay, several top Filipino politicians were financed by the CIA, among them President Diosdado Macapagal and his vice president, Emmanuel Pelaez, later Cory Aquino's ambassador to Washington. Ninoy was proud to have had a connection with the CIA, contending however that he had worked "with" rather than "for" the agency. The affiliation represented a link to the United States—a badge of distinction.

But Filipinos also recoil from tarnishing their nationalist image by too close an association with the Americans. They seem to be trapped in a tangle of contradictions. History is responsible. Despite their own vague past, the Filipinos might have forged their national personality had they been compelled to fight for freedom—as they were indeed doing in their conflict against Spain. By acceding to their aspirations for sovereignty so soon after conquest, the United States spared them a long struggle for independence. But, in a sense, their hopes were fulfilled too easily. America's acquiescence to their ambitions deflated the élan of their early nationalism, leaving them confused and ambivalent. From then on, their attitudes toward the United States vacillated between imitation and resentment, subservience and defiance, adulation and contempt, love and hate. The same dichotomy continues to trouble them, as it did Quezon back in the 1920s. Once, in a fit of nationalist passion, he asserted: "I would prefer a government run like hell by Filipinos to one run like heaven by Americans." On another occasion, incensed that the benevolence of the United States was puncturing his nationalist pretensions, he exploded: "Damn the Americans! Why don't they tyrannize us more?"

3

An Enduring Presence

The impact of the West is still engraved on its former colonies around the world. Apart from the Casbah, Algiers is a southern French city, and Nairobi, Kenya, bears the traces of an English town. Djakarta, Indonesia, with its canals and step-roofed brick houses, faintly recalls its onetime Dutch masters. But in no place is the imperial legacy more alive than in Manila, where America's presence is almost as dynamic now as it was during the days of U.S. rule.

The suburbs, a blight of fast-food franchises and used-car lots, stretch endlessly to nowhere, like the outskirts of Los Angeles. Aside from the armed security guards at their gates, testimony to Manila's staggering crime rate, affluent residential districts resemble Beverly Hills. The fanciest of them, Forbes Park, is named for a vintage American governor. Taft Avenue and Harrison Plaza also remember American colonial governors. Streets honor Presidents McKinley, Wilson and the two Roosevelts, as well as John D. Rockefeller, Henry Ford, Thomas Edison and Alexander Graham Bell. Bridges commemorate General MacArthur and William Atkinson Jones, an obscure

Virginia congressman who in 1916 sponsored the legislation that pledged eventual independence for the Philippines.

The aforementioned statehood party claims 5 million members. Nearly every Filipino seems to have a relative in California, Illinois or New Jersey. One hundred thousand candidates apply every year for the 400 slots open to Filipinos in the U.S. Navy. A captured Communist rebel escapes from jail and flees abroad—to San Francisco rather than Hanoi, Beijing or Moscow. In a reverse psychological twist, a young insurgent on the island of Negros explained to me through an interpreter how America's pervasive influence had prompted him to join the insurrection. "My ambition as a kid was to be like an American. We'd been taught in school that the Americans were our saviors, that they brought us democracy. When I saw cowboy-and-Indian movies, I always rooted for the cowboys. I preferred American-style clothes. Americans were rich, handsome and superior. Jesus Christ and the Virgin Mary looked like Americans, with their white skins and long noses. I degraded Filipinos because they were ugly, with flat noses and brown skins. But I was also ugly. I wasn't a good student, and could not speak English well. Then I began to realize that I would never become like an American, and I started to hate America."

Every young Filipino dreams of attending college, and diploma mills grind out worthless degrees in law, accountancy and public relations. But Ivy League credentials are coveted, especially in business administration—the passport to a fat job in Makati, Manila's financial district. In the summer of 1980, Ninoy telephoned me from a Texas hospital, where he was recovering from heart surgery. Marcos had released him from prison for the operation on condition that he return home afterward. Having agreed, Ninoy was now contemplating ways to stay in America without violating his pledge. "Marcos can't resist if I go to Harvard," he mused, figuring that the prestige of Cambridge would melt even his implacable enemy—who himself claimed to have been once accepted at Harvard. Ninoy proved to be correct. A fellowship was arranged, and he spent the next three years in Boston.

American English Spoken Here

Nothing illustrates America's impact as vividly as the widespread use of American English. Candidates campaign in English, delivering florid orations in a rhetoric reminiscent of vintage American politicians. English is employed in the courts and in government agencies. Even Communist insurgents rely on English versions of Marx and Mao Zedong to denounce America. The government has been striving for decades to promote Tagalog, renamed Pilipino, as the national language. But only 30 percent of Filipinos speak Tagalog, mainly in Luzon. About the same proportion speaks Cebuano, the language of the Visayas, the islands that sprawl across the center of the archipelago.

Spanish priests, fearing that the natives might become "uppity" if taught Spanish, themselves learned local languages and dialects. But the pioneer American teachers considered it their mission to make English the common tongue, and their students cooperated eagerly. Proficiency in English soon became a mark of distinction among Filipinos, many of whom looked back with veneration on their American education. The journalist and diplomat Carlos P. Romulo accepted the Pulitzer Prize in 1942 for a newspaper series on Asia with the words: "The real winner is . . . Hattie Grove, who taught a small Filipino pupil to value the beauty of the English language."

American teachers introduced baseball as an antidote to cockfighting, the national Filipino addiction. The *Manila Times,* an American newspaper, wrote early in the century that baseball was "more than a game, a regenerating influence and power for good." The effort partly succeeded. Filipinos became avid fans, and their media detail major league action in the United States, but cockfighting remains the countrywide diversion.

Superb entertainers, Filipinos adapted to the arrival of the Americans by dropping the *zarzuela,* a Spanish music hall, in favor of vaudeville, or *bodabil*—its performers billed as the "Filipino Sophie Tucker," the "Filipino Al Jolson" or the "Filipino Fred Astaire." Subsequent years spawned Filipino Bing Crosbys, Glenn Millers, Guy Lombardos, Elvis Presleys, Barbra Streisands. Rock groups with names like Hot Dog and the

Boyfriends appeared as clones of the Grateful Dead and Led Zeppelin—though they slowed their beat to a tropical tempo. One of Manila's liveliest amateur jazz bands is the Executive Combo, comprised of a half-dozen businessmen, lawyers and government officials. Their hero is Duke Ellington, their theme song is "Take the A Train" and their leader, who doubles on the piano and drums, is Raul S. Manglapus, the foreign secretary in Cory Aquino's cabinet. His reverence for American jazz notwithstanding, he also composed a satirical musical entitled "Yankee Panky" as an assault against U.S. policy toward the Philippines.

A Question of Values

While the United States left a more durable imprint on the Philippines than the Europeans did on their colonies, the impact was only superficial. Nevertheless, both Americans and Filipinos have diligently clung to the illusion that they share a common public philosophy—when, in reality, their values are dramatically dissimilar.

America's imperial effort started out as an exercise in "self-duplication," as the historian Glenn May has put it. Taft went to Manila with the preconceived notion that the Filipinos were unsuited to govern themselves, and his first impressions only confirmed his prejudice. "The great mass of the people are ignorant and superstitious," he observed, while the few men "who have any education that deserves the name" were mostly "intriguing politicians, without the slightest moral stamina, and nothing but personal interests to gratify." They were "oriental in their duplicity" and, he estimated, it might take a century of training "before they shall ever realize what Anglo-Saxon liberty is." However, he declared, the United States had a "sacred duty" to Americanize them. With that, he launched his program to instill in them the values that had made America the greatest society on earth: integrity, civic responsibility and respect for impersonal institutions. No matter that the United States at the time was itself riddled with corruption, racism and appalling economic disparities. America's mission was to export its virtues, not its sins. Through patient political tutelage, Taft said, the

Filipinos could be taught "the possibility of honest administration." Over time, realizing the limitations of their influence, U.S. officials reluctantly accommodated to Filipino traditions. Yet they continued to claim that America was transforming the Philippines into a "showcase of democracy" rather than admit that their effort had fallen short of expectations.

Their task was daunting from the outset. They found in the Philippines a society based on a complicated and often baffling web of real and ritual kinship ties—the antithesis of the American ideal of a nation of citizens united in their devotion to the welfare of all.

Blood Ties and Extended Families

Again history explains the phenomenon: Before the arrival of the Spanish, the Filipinos belonged to no social group larger than the village, which was in fact their family. Catholic priests spread through the countryside, further sanctifying the family by exhorting the Filipinos to identify with the Holy Family—God the powerful father, the compassionate Virgin mother and Christ, whose suffering and humiliation matched their own misery. The friars also introduced the Catholic custom of godparenthood, which fused with the pre-Hispanic practice of blood covenants with tribal allies to create a network of *compadres*, or ritual relatives. The sponsors of a child's baptism, for example, became the ceremonial kin of its parents, and the ritual family could expand to astonishing dimensions as well through weddings, funerals and confirmations. Calculating the possible permutations, Filipinos outdo Chaucer's man from St. Ives. Historian Theodore Friend has reckoned that a father with five children who enlists four sponsors, each with a family of four, can theoretically weave a fabric of nearly 500 kin. The system has lost its original religious character as Filipinos, out of expediency, forge secular links with professional partners, army comrades, schoolmates.

Filipinos are absorbed into these alliances from infancy. Children, always invited to celebrations attended by real and fictive relatives, learn to feel comfortable at an early age in the warm fold of parents, brothers, sisters, uncles, aunts, cousins and ritual kinfolk. But they also learn as they grow up that these ties impose reciprocal responsibilities that must be observed to avoid the worst of all fates: exclusion from the extended family.

Personal rather than institutional relationships guide Filipinos, making them less sensitive to the rules of society than to the opinions of their real or ritual kin, whose esteem they must win and retain. Hence their obsession with *hiya,* a Tagalog term that conveys the supremely important concept of "face." To behave decorously toward family and friends, to display respect for an elder, kindness toward an underling, deference toward a superior—all show exemplary hiya and are ways to gain face. Failure to exhibit these qualities is *walang hiya,* to act shamelessly and thus lose face in the eyes of others. Equally vital is *utang na loob,* the "debt of gratitude" that Filipinos are ethically expected to repay in return for favors, lest they be guilty of walang hiya. A Filipino who renders services piles up credit for the future, since those he has assisted become indebted to him.

Compadres

At its best, this mutual obligation pattern is an ideal social-security mechanism. Filipinos help to raise their siblings and later care for their aged parents. If they become wealthy or rise to high office, they are required to support their relatives or find them government jobs. Even the poorest scrape to aid their more indigent kin, and no house is so humble that it lacks a spot for an unfortunate relative. Thousands of Filipinos rely on remittances from their children in the United States. Four hundred thousand Filipinos are employed abroad, mostly in lonely places like Saudi Arabia, Bahrain and Kuwait. Working on contract for two or three years as technicians, nurses, drivers and clerks, they send an estimated $1 billion a year home—a sum equal to one fourth of the country's earnings from exports. Numbers of women serve as domestics in Singapore and Hong Kong, many ending up as prostitutes. Guaranteed the hospitality of cousins and in-laws, Filipinos travel around the islands for only the cost of air fare. They take cheap charter flights to America, then sponge off an uncle in San Diego, a sister in Chicago or a nephew in Boston. The *compadrazgo* system also protects Filipinos, who out of suspicion and fear divide their relationships into "we" and "they." A compadre is supposedly trustworthy because he has ritually sworn an oath of eternal fidelity. But the system is not foolproof. The fact that Ninoy Aquino belonged to Marcos's college fraternity—and was by definition a compadre whom he privately called brother—did not prevent the dictator from imprisoning him for eight years.

The Philippines also owes its worst abuses to the strong blood and ceremonial alliances, whose mutual obligations spawn pervasive corruption. Greed alone is not the motive. Public figures rely on their real and ritual kin to win elected or appointed office, and once in authority, they then must reimburse their supporters with government contracts, tax breaks, import and export licenses and other favors, both legal and illicit. The recipients in turn kick back a proportion of their profits to the cooperative officials, and so the cycle of graft and fraud becomes normal practice.

'Good Crooks, Bad Crooks'

Reflecting on his career as a mayor, province governor and senator, Ninoy once reckoned that he had amassed some 10,000 compadres who would recruit their compadres and the compadres of their compadres to work for him during elections. In exchange, he expedited their business deals, found them jobs, even paid to send their children to private schools. "An American politician kisses babies, but here we finance their education," he quipped—leaving it to me to guess that he had occult sources of money. For all her own integrity, Cory Aquino has not been able to restrain one of her brothers and his wife from engaging in shady transactions. Marcos, himself personally abstemious, pillaged the country partly in hopes of founding a dynasty for his indolent son Bong Bong. He also granted his cronies and army generals lucrative monopolies to recompense them for helping his rise to power. Filipinos, accustomed to venal leaders, might have forgiven him had not his profligacy plunged the nation into bankruptcy. President Carlos P. Garcia hardly caused a ripple in

1960 when he defended a fraudulent aide on the grounds that he was simply "providing for the future of his family." Not long before, José Avelino, a prominent legislator, dared to state openly what most of his colleagues believed privately. One of the rare politicians ever censured for corruption, he urged the president at the time, Elpidio Quirino, not to press the charge against him. "What are we in power for? We are not hypocrites. Why should we pretend to be saints when in reality we are not? When Jesus Christ died on the cross, he made a distinction between good crooks and bad crooks. We can be good crooks."

The elaborate kinship system accounts as well for the social rigidity of the Philippines. Bishop Francisco Claver, a professor of sociology at the Ateneo de Manila, a Jesuit university, maintains that the country's values have hardly changed since pre-Spanish times. Families, he explained to me, are really ancient tribes in modern disguise, with the father the uncontested chief and everyone else occupying a designated niche in the pyramidal structure. "So Filipinos have been taught since childhood to respect authority, not to rebel or to question, and they are passive, even fatalistic. The poor believe that they are destined to be poor, and the rich assume that their wealth was ordained. Climbing from the lower classes to the peak of the pyramid is impossible. An Abraham Lincoln, a man of humble origin, could never become president of the Philippines." A Filipino journalist phrased it more succinctly: "It's not what you are and what you can do, but who you are, your name and your connections."

Feudalism and the 60 Families

The calcified structure approaches feudalism in the rural areas. Plantations have belonged to the same dynasties for generations, and tenants can trace their roots on the property back to their grandfathers and great-grandfathers. Besides furnishing the sharecroppers with loans, seeds and tools in return for a percentage of the harvest, the landowners preside at their baptisms, weddings and funerals—thereby indebting the peasants both financially and morally. The local lords invariably control the mayor, police chief and regional army commander, and many maintain private security forces equipped with modern weapons and trained by foreign mercenaries. Many also subsidize vigilante groups, partly as a defense against insurgents but also to fight their vendettas. I once spent an evening with a banana planter at his house near the city of Davao, on the southern island of Mindanao. We drove out from town in a bullet-proof van and into a floodlit compound, its walls and watchtowers manned by guards with machine guns. "Normal precautions," he said of the setup.

A single statistic is illustrative: The top one fifth of the Philippine population receives half the country's income. An American Jesuit scholar, Father John Doherty, has estimated that 60 families control the Philippine economy. They have also dominated the political scene from the start of the U.S. colonial era to the Aquino government. Despite their Americanized hoopla, elections are actually contests between rival clans, and the "showcase of democracy" is a facade that only transparently conceals the rule of an elite that has consistently refused to surrender its privileges. The latest agrarian reform legislation, like numbers of apparently progressive land-tenure laws already on the books, is a tissue of loopholes.

No wonder, then, that a Communist insurgency that began with a handful of rebels in the early 1970s has since spread throughout the archipelago. Cory Aquino, whose ordeal during her husband's imprisonment by Marcos had earned her the sympathy of human rights groups like Amnesty International, has ironically become their target by sanctioning anti-Communist vigilantes and failing to prosecute alleged Philippine army abuses. The charges against her military establishment, she has retorted, have "shown up to be total lies." But even if she did attempt to try offenders, it is doubtful that she could rotate the wheels of justice. Clogged by incompetence and corruption, the courts function slowly or not at all. Defendants rely on their families or compadres to hire thugs to harass, abduct and even murder witnesses. Frustrated by the paralyzed legal system, Filipinos regularly resort to violence as a means of arbitration, knowing that the chances of being arrested, much less punished, are slim. Mayors and municipal officials live in constant fear, and no political candidate would campaign without a squad of bodyguards. Not a single soldier or policeman was convicted of a human rights violation committed after Cory took office—or, for that matter, during the Marcos regime. Years of hearings and investigations failed to apprehend Ninoy's assassins.

Traditional values have meanwhile shaded the attitudes of Filipinos toward the United States in complex and subtle ways. Many Filipinos, recalling America's schools, liberal political tutelage and early pledge of independence, were motivated by feelings of gratitude toward the United States. And, loyal to the concept of utang na loob, they fulfilled the debt of honor by fighting alongside Americans at Bataan and Corregidor, and by joining guerrilla movements to resist the Japanese during World War II. The shared agony ingrained in them the idea of a family tie between the United States and the Philippines. As Quezon's compadre, MacArthur perceived as few Americans did their personal approach to the relationship. But the United States, its foreign policy predicated on self-interest rather than sentimentality, ignored their view. As a result, the Filipinos were disappointed and dismayed when, following the war, the Americans gave them far less economic aid than they granted Japan, the common enemy.

The Bases Issue

Filipinos, in recurrent surges of nationalism, focused their resentment against the U.S. bases in the Philippines, the most visible sign of America's residual presence in the archipelago. And the issue promised to test their ties to the United States for years to come.

The Subic Naval Base and Clark Air Base, America's two largest overseas military installations, had long been of mutual value to both the Philippines and the United States. The "rent" paid for the bases, disguised as various forms of American aid, represented only a part of their importance to the Philippine economy—which, in the aftermath of Marcos's profligacy, desperately needed all the help it could muster. By 1988, the bases

Villagers watch as members of the Communist New People's Army train. President Aquino has been unsuccessful in curbing insurgency.

employed some 70,000 Filipinos, more than the nation's 10 leading corporations combined, contributing more than $1 billion a year in revenues, double the total amount of foreign investment in the country. The bases also earned the Philippines more income than any single one of its exports. But the United States was getting its money's worth. Clark field was no longer as vital as it had been during the decades following World War II when missiles supplanted aircraft as intercontinental weapons, and planes themselves developed long-range capabilities. By contrast, the U.S. Navy cherished Subic Bay for its enormous storage facilities as well as its loyal, skilled and relatively inexpensive Filipino labor force, many of whose fathers and grandfathers had worked there before them, and to relocate the base would have been costly. For American strategists, however, a crucial consideration was the presence of the installations as the symbol of a continued U.S. role in the Pacific—particularly in the wake of the defeat in Vietnam. It was a perception shared by China, Japan and the nations of Southeast Asia, all of whom regarded the American fleet to be a counterweight to growing Soviet strength in the region. The Japanese, almost totally dependent on imported oil, saw the Philippine bases as indispensable to the security of their sea-lanes to the Indian Ocean and the Middle East.

Surveys have repeatedly shown a majority of Filipinos to be in favor of the U.S. bases. The attitude has reflected their awareness of the economic value of the bases, combined with the pro-American sentiment that has long pervaded the society. I had been prepared to believe the conventional wisdom that held that sympathy for the United States was concentrated mainly in the older generation of Filipinos who nostalgically remembered America's benevolent colonial rule and liberation of the Philippines from the Japanese during World War II. But a poll conducted in 1986 indicated that 76 percent of Filipino high-school editors supported the U.S. bases. The statistic seemed to contradict the mounting clamor against the bases then consuming Manila's vocal elite—which swelled into strident chorus during the years that followed. In fact, it illustrated once more that a few Manila politicians and newspaper columnists exert disproportionate influence over the Philippine government compared to the opinion of the population.

Spasms of nationalist passions directed against the United States had always served Filipinos as a convenient distraction from their internal problems. Marcos had kept the fervor in check, reserving for himself the right to juggle the bases issue as a device to extract concessions from the United States. By dismantling his regime, however, Cory Aquino restored Manila politics to its rough-and-tumble style—and, in the process, the bases question became fair game for every public figure. She remained silent except to say that she intended to keep her "options open" until 1991, when the lease on the installations expired. But discussions aimed at reaching an interim agreement opened in the summer of 1987, and it quickly appeared to U.S. diplomats involved in the talks that their Filipino counterparts, eager to demonstrate their nationalism, might be swept by their own rhetoric into a position that precluded compromise. Or as one of the American negotiators told me, "They may be painting themselves into a corner." Stealing the initiative from Cory, the

Philippine senate voted to ban nuclear weapons from the country. The decision, if upheld by the entire legislature, would render the bases inoperative.

End of the 'Special Relationship'?

Inconsistencies predictably clouded the subject. Raul Manglapus, foreign secretary and chief Filipino negotiator, asserted from the start that "we must slay the father image"—the metaphor signifying that the Philippines could not mature as a nation as long as the bases remained as a reminder of the American colonial era. On the other hand, he hinted that he might concede if the United States raised its aid package to $1.2 billion a year from the $180 million it was then paying. "If the Americans can't afford it," he said, "they should go." But Father Joaquin Bernas, a Jesuit commentator, remarked that "you don't put a dollar tag on dignity," and others, echoing the same theme, called for "cutting the umbilical cord" and severing "the rope that strangles our growth as a nation." Some Filipinos also contended that a "mini-Marshall plan" of $10 billion in aid for the Philippines, proposed by a group of U.S. congressmen, was actually a trap designed to secure the bases. Amando Doronila, the scholarly editor of *The Manila Chronicle,* who had earlier forecast a settlement, finally concluded in June 1987 that "at some stage— maybe sooner than later—the bases must go." The "special relationship" between America and the Philippines was finished, he wrote: "Of all the nations with which the United States has close ties, there is nothing special about us, no matter whether many of us think otherwise."

His fondness for Cory Aquino notwithstanding, Secretary of State Shultz entered the debate with a virtual ultimatum. Unless the Filipinos toned down their demands, he cautioned, "we'll have to find some other place to have our ships and planes, because we only want to be at a place where we have an ally that wants us there." Admiral William J. Crowe Jr., chairman of the Joint Chiefs of Staff, was equally adamant, telling me in an interview: "We don't want to be where we're not wanted." The warnings were not entirely a bluff. Pentagon planners had indeed been weighing alternatives, among them the Pacific islands of Guam, Tinian and Saipan, all U.S. possessions untrammeled by the question of sovereignty.

An agreement was ultimately signed in Washington on October 17, 1988, but the bases issue, whatever its long-range solution, threatened to confront the Filipinos with a dilemma that transcended the problem of the bases themselves. Despite their nationalist rhetoric, an American withdrawal would symbolize a family schism for most Filipinos. Should the United States remain, their effort to reinforce their national identity would be retarded—as it has been since the Americans first landed in 1898.

In Search of a Distinct National Character

A far more critical challenge facing the Filipinos, though, was the renovation of their society. In July 1968, Ninoy Aquino depicted his nation's plight in *Foreign Affairs,* and the portrait still rings true. "The Philippines is a land of traumatic contrasts," he wrote. "Here is a land in which a few are spectacularly rich while the masses remain abjectly poor. Here is a land where freedom and its blessings are a reality for the minority and an illusion for the many. Here is a land consecrated to democracy but run by an entrenched plutocracy. Here is a land of privilege and rank—a republic dedicated to equality but mired in an archaic system of caste." Its government was "financially almost bankrupt," its state agencies "ridden by debts and honeycombed with graft," its industries "in pathetic distress." There was "no organized, no methodical overall economic planning," but only "haphazard attempts to modernize," confused by a "multiplicity of cravings and concerns." So Filipinos were "depressed and dispirited . . . without purpose and without discipline . . . sapped of confidence, hope and will." The fault was mainly theirs. "They profess love of country, but love themselves—individually—more."

Like today's nationalists, Ninoy also blamed Spain and the United States for remolding the Filipinos "in their own image" and depriving them of their "soul"—an experience that had left them "bewildered" about their identity. "They were an Asian people not Asian in the eyes of their fellow Asians, not Western in the eyes of the West." Only by "bold efforts to break away from the fetters of the past," he urged, could they develop a distinct national character.

Few countries, however, have been more heavily shackled by the past than the Philippines. And, after one of the longest continuous periods of Western imperial rule in world history, Filipinos are still freighted with what they lament as their "colonial mentality." But they are doubly dependent: on their own oligarchy and on America.

4

Revolution: The Overthrow
of President Marcos

"D ear God, let it not be me," Cory pleaded in the summer of
1985, flinching at the challenge, when she was increasingly
cited as the only person who could mend the split opposition to
Marcos. "I didn't want to be the candidate," she recalled to me
later. "I'm very private and wasn't meant to be at center stage."
But she canvased family members and friends—and, begging for
divine guidance, she prayed "as I'd never prayed before." The
pressure on her intensified after Marcos scheduled the election. If
she abstained, she knew, the likely contender would be Salvador
H. Laurel, a routine politician of dubious repute. A priest,
couching the issue in moral terms she grasped, was decisive. In
this struggle between good and evil, he said, she alone embodied
the values of "truth, freedom and justice" that could beat Marcos.
She agreed to run on condition that her supporters compile a draft
petition containing a million signatures. They did—and, after a
day of meditation at a convent near Manila, she declared.

Now, in need of political counsel, she consulted the country's shrewdest politician: Jaime Cardinal Sin. He advised her to work with Laurel, but she would have him only as her vice-president. Sin then urged Laurel, who had presidential hopes, to accept the number-two slot. "Cory is more popular than you are," Sin flatly told him. "Make the sacrifice, or Marcos will win." After waffling for weeks, Laurel conceded.

Cory had showed herself to be tougher than she appeared. But she was ingenuous in an interview with *The New York Times* in December 1985. The newspaper's Manila correspondent, Seth Mydans, brought along the hardnosed executive editor, A. M. "Abe" Rosenthal, who happened to be in town. Untutored, Cory nattered away, occasionally asking the amiable Mydans how to answer the questions, or replying as though she were thinking aloud. If elected, she would "probably" try Marcos for Ninoy's murder. She favored the "removal" of the U.S. bases at some future date, preferring instead to bring the Philippines into a "zone of neutrality," and would open a "dialogue" with the Communists, many of whom merely "want justice." As for her presidential program: "The only thing I can really offer the Filipino people is my sincerity."

The Washington conservatives cackled at her naïveté. Worse yet, Rosenthal returned home to decry her incompetence. His judgment strengthened Reagan's bias against her and even left an imprint on Shultz, whose faith in Marcos had by then faded. Two months later, when Cory was the only alternative to the crumbling Marcos regime, Shultz still recalled at a key meeting that Rosenthal had pictured her as "vacant." But her flop in *The New York Times* prompted her American friends to pitch in to repair the damage.

The U.S. embassy also lent her subtle support, such as advice on how to focus on American public opinion. The U.S. Agency for International Development partly financed NAMFREL, the National Committee for Free Elections, which was to help her by signaling Marcos's skulduggery at the polls. Her sympathizers were bolstered, too, by the real or illusory belief that Ambassador Stephen W. Bosworth would ultimately defend her. A tactful diplomat, he was restrained in public, but Manila's flourishing rumor mill quoted him as having pledged privately, "If Marcos tries to stay in power, we'll disintegrate him in 30 days."

For the U.S. news media the event was irresistible: a morality play in an Americanized setting with the principal characters speaking English. The major American television networks each fielded several crews along with such stars as Tom Brokaw and Peter Jennings, and they could have been back home. The candidates knew all about prime time and ratings—so much so that Marcos insisted on being interviewed on CBS only by Dan Rather. He and Cory craved attention in the United States in the realization that American validation made them credible to the Filipinos, who distrusted their own news media. Many Filipinos suspected that Marcos had faked his war record, for example, but the story only became true after it appeared in *The New York Times*—and was reprinted by Manila's opposition newspapers. The correspondents also served as witnesses, particularly for Cory, whose staff directed them to areas where Marcos's goons might disrupt the voting. To Marcos, conversely, journalists were snooping nuisances, yet he too needed them to deliver his message.

A Charismatic Campaigner

As the campaign gathered momentum, it was plain that much of the old oligarchy dispossessed by Marcos had swung to Cory. Rich Manila matrons garbed in tailored yellow blouses answered telephones and served as typists at her headquarters or put their chauffeured cars at her disposal. Despite threats from Marcos, companies loaned her their private aircraft to tour the provinces and poured a total of some $6 million into her coffers. The clergy openly backed her. One Sunday morning, at a church on Negros, the parish priest informed me that she would receive the collection plate. I sensed, traveling with her, that she was altering the pattern of Philippine politics. Elections had traditionally been races between rival clans, with voters obedient to their patrons. Now, it seemed, Cory was in direct communion with the people, projecting an aura of sanctity that almost mesmerized devout Filipinos. Her Joan of Arc image, though a tired stereotype, was nevertheless real.

Marcos's few campaign outings, by contrast, were lugubrious. Visibly ill, he had to be lifted bodily onto platforms, and his cracked voice was slurred and often inaudible. He was incontinent, a grim task for his handlers.

Election day, February 7, 1986, was marred by the usual cases of stolen ballot boxes, intimidation and even killings, almost all of it by Marcos's thugs. The serious cheating, though, came in adding the votes. Under U.S. pressure, Marcos had allowed NAMFREL, the independent monitor, to tabulate the results in tandem with COMELEC, the official Commission on Elections. Marcos wanted a credibly slim margin of victory, not a suspicious landslide. So, while NAMFREL reported Cory ahead, COMELEC delayed the count to enable Marcos to tailor the total. Republican Senator Richard G. Lugar's 20 U.S. observers immediately smelled fraud, as did the platoons of State Department and CIA men brought in especially to track the race. A night after the polls closed, 30 computer technicians tallying the vote dramatized Marcos's sham by fleeing the COMELEC headquarters for the refuge of a church—contending that the figures showing Cory in the lead were being discarded.

A State Department task force in Washington, keeping an around-the-clock watch on the Philippines, provided Reagan with massive evidence of Marcos's abuses, but Reagan preferred his own eccentric sources: Nancy fed him information that she was receiving by telephone from Imelda. Donald Regan, his chief of staff, who knew nothing about the Philippines, nevertheless pressed him to stick with Marcos. Their bias was shared by CIA director William Casey, despite the messages of his men in the field.

Lugar, perceiving that Reagan was prepared to recognize a Marcos victory, warned him that Marcos was "cooking the results." Reagan replied by mentioning a television segment he had seen of Filipinos destroying ballots and identified them as Cory's campaigners—when, as it later turned out, they were Marcos supporters. At a rare news conference, Reagan admitted that violence had been "evident" and conceded to the "possibility of fraud" in the election, but he suggested that "it could have been

... occurring on both sides." His primary concern in the Philippines were the bases, not political liberty. "I don't know of anything more important than those bases," he emphasized.

Flabbergasted, Lugar refuted Reagan, his party leader, telling an audience in Indianapolis, "The president was misinformed." Other politicians, Republicans and Democrats alike, echoed his dismay. They were largely reacting to constituents who had seen the faraway campaign on television, fallen in love with Cory and shared her passion to make good prevail over evil. Americans were rediscovering that the Philippines had once been a U.S. colony and, infused with renewed missionary zeal, they felt it their duty to extend their benevolence to their former protégés.

Cory was furious that Reagan equated her with the wicked Marcos. She vented her anger on Bosworth—who himself was devastated. He and his embassy staff had bombarded Washington with proof of Marcos's fraud, only to be shattered by Reagan's disregard.

Frustrated, Bosworth shouted over the telephone to his colleagues at the State Department. "But they were just as horrified," he recollected, "and I was like the minister preaching to the choir." Shultz soon called him and, in his bland voice, said: "Okay, you've made your point. Now relax. We'll try to fix it." He did. Reagan had gone to his Santa Barbara ranch, and Shultz dunned him by telephone with details of Marcos's deceit. On February 15, Reagan finally acknowledged publicly that the "widespread fraud and violence" had been "perpetrated largely" by Marcos's side. A few hours later, Marcos announced victory— and the first foreign envoy to congratulate him was the Soviet ambassador. Cory promptly claimed success—credibly, according to the CIA's estimates.

Habib Mission

Philip Habib, the diplomatic troubleshooter, now plunged into the confusion. A Brooklynite of Lebanese origin, he was a veteran of nearly 40 years in the State Department—an ethnic rarity in the patrician corps. He had risen to become ambassador to South Korea and later under secretary of state before a severe heart attack retired him. Still energetic, he undertook special missions. He had always prided himself on his candor and was even blunter in retirement—figuring, as he put it, that he had "paid his dues." On February 9, two days after the Philippine election, Shultz interrupted Habib's golf game in Florida to ask him to go to Manila. Habib detested the Marcoses, but he accepted the job—which, as he subsequently described it to me, was "simply to assess the situation." Shultz's real purpose in sending him was to gain time to enable the Administration to resolve the deadlock. Habib, however, was too dynamic to play a passive role.

Landing in Manila on February 15, he found himself in a swirl. More than 100 Catholic bishops had just declared that Marcos's "fraudulent" attempt to retain power "has no moral basis." Then Cory staged a huge rally in the Luneta, appealing for civil disobedience to unseat Marcos. Habib calmed her jitters by reassuring her that he had not come to urge her to compromise. Marcos, whom he saw, claimed to have won the election. For six days Habib interviewed more than 100 politicians, priests, educators, businessmen—and two journalists, Robert Shaplen of *The New Yorker* and me. He was particularly impressed by Juan Ponce Enrile, who seemed to be distancing himself from Marcos and, Habib felt, might soon "reveal his hand." By February 22, as he prepared to depart, Habib had concluded: "Cory had won the election and deserved our support. Marcos was finished, and we ought to offer him asylum in the United States."

Before boarding his U.S. Air Force plane for the flight home, Habib intuitively told an American embassy officer to tell Bosworth, "Something's going to break."

The Role of Enrile

Lean and leathery at 62, Enrile owed his wealth and status to a nimble mind, a sense of timing and patronage. He had been born illegitimate in the mountains of north Luzon and was later adopted by his father, a noted Manila attorney, who sent him to Harvard Law School. Enrile joined Marcos in 1965 and became his defense minister five years afterward, meanwhile piling up a fortune as Eduardo Cojuangco's associate in the coconut monopoly. But he felt increasingly estranged as Marcos placed the armed forces under General Fabian C. Ver. Soon Enrile discovered that Ver was planning to have him murdered—a fate he escaped when his bodyguards located and liquidated the suspected killer. Enrile's fears also mounted when he learned that Cojuangco, possibly working with Ver, was gunning for him as well. In 1984, Cojuangco hired three Israeli mercenaries to train his private army of nearly 2,000 men. Ninoy's death had alarmed Enrile. Until then, he told me later, assassinating a "man of any consequence" was simply not done. Now "nobody was safe."

Enrile formed his own force with a core of some 30 young officers. Starting in late 1983, he secretly imported crates of Israeli weapons along with two retired British commandos to teach his men deceptive tactics. The young Filipino officers, many of them trained in the United States, were serious soldiers—though one, Colonel Gregorio "Gringo" Honasan, was a showman whose stunts included parachute jumping while encoiled by his pet python. As professionals, they lamented the favoritism, incompetence and corruption that pervaded the armed forces, crippling their ability to check the Communist insurgents. Rex Robles, a navy captain, wept as he later described conditions to me: "Our men were fighting in shorts and rubber sandals, without uniforms, boots, even canteens. They were dying for lack of doctors, nurses, medicines—while Marcos's generals stole millions."

Plotting Marcos's Overthrow

In March 1985, the young officers organized the Reform the Armed Forces Movement, or RAM, and soon began to plot. They outlined options ranging from the "benign," like urging Marcos to change, to the "naughty," such as abducting him and forcing him to quit. Eventually they agreed on a "naughty" plan: to oust him and set up a committee including Enrile, Cory, Cardinal Sin and Lieutenant General Fidel Ramos, the constabulary chief, as a transition back to normal rule. But Marcos's election announcement in November 1985 jolted them. They could not move without appearing to be thwarting the democratic process.

Delaying their plot, they vowed to act should Marcos cheat. Whatever the outcome, their choice for eventual president was Enrile, not Cory.

Like boys on a lark, they noisily conspired over beer in the vast lobby of the Peninsula Hotel, and soon all Manila, including Ver and Bosworth, were in the know. Bosworth reckoned that Ver could easily crush an attempted coup or might preempt it. In either event, Marcos would reimpose martial law under the guise of restoring order, and Reagan would probably approve the action. Bosworth warned both Ver and the RAM officers to do nothing. So the two sides played "bluff" during the early weeks of 1985, as Robles recalled. "We leaked to the press that we were about to move, and they did the same. It was a matter of who blinked first."

Marcos's election chicanery finally spurred the plotters to schedule a coup for the early hours of Sunday, February 23, the feast of Saint Lazarus. Their plan was to attack the Malacañang and seize Marcos—but, above all, not kill him. They alerted Ramos, whose men were vital. Cardinal Sin, obliquely informed, obliquely blessed them. Cory, in the dark, was going with her brother to Cebu to campaign for civil disobedience, and they advised him to keep her there.

Suddenly there was a hitch. On February 20, Marcos had arrested four rebel confederates in his entourage, and they talked. The RAM officers heard of the arrest two days later, when they also learned that other comrades had been picked up. It was now the day before the coup, and Colonel Honasan warned Enrile that an attack against the palace would be suicide. He had also been told that they were about to be arrested. Hastily revising plans, they decided to retreat to Camp Aguinaldo, a large Manila military compound and site of Enrile's defense ministry, and appeal to other army elements for support.

At six o'clock on the evening of February 22, Enrile arrived at the camp, a bulletproof vest under his olive drab windbreaker. He was joined by Ramos, an undemonstrative West Point graduate. They initially had only 200 men—no match for Marcos's legions. Enrile first telephoned Bosworth to tell him of their move.

Bosworth informed Washington, then began a series of calls to Marcos, urging him not to employ force. Enrile also called Cardinal Sin to say, "I'll be dead in an hour." Soon, mobbed by correspondents, Enrile held a televised news conference in which he recognized Cory as the election winner—revealing that he himself faked nearly 400,000 votes for Marcos in his own region. He went on to confess to other duplicity, including the phony ambush in 1972 that gave Marcos the pretext to declare martial law.

People Power

Other soldiers drifted into the camp. Within hours, too, thousands of people swarmed around Epifanio de los Santos Avenue, known as Edsa, a broad boulevard running past the compound. Hawkers quickly poured in to peddle food, drinks, cigarettes and Ninoy souvenirs. More disaffected troops arrived, and the crowd swelled. Ramos shifted to Camp Crame, a more defensible installation across the boulevard, where Enrile later joined him. At nine o'clock that night, the irrepressible Cardinal Sin spoke on Radio Veritas, appealing for support of "our two good friends," Enrile and Ramos. Cory, hearing news of the revolt in Cebu, was convinced that Marcos would swiftly wipe it out. The U.S. consul offered her refuge aboard an American Navy frigate anchored in the port. Instead she went to a nearby convent to wait, watch and pray. She telephoned Cardinal Sin, who optimistically told her, "This may be the miracle we've been expecting."

If so, providence was assisted by clandestine American intervention. Rebel helicopters were allowed to refuel and rearm at Clark field, the U.S. commander noting afterward that technically the base belonged to the Philippines. Defense Secretary Caspar W. Weinberger maintained later that the choppers were helping to "avert bloodshed," though one fired rockets at the Malacañang palace. The American military mission in Manila intercepted messages between the two sides, ostensibly to "make sure that they understood each other," but also to slip intelligence to the rebels. A team of U.S. experts tapped into Ver's secret radio net and furnished the dissidents with his orders to his men. On Sunday morning, when Marcos's troops smashed the Radio Veritas transmitter, CIA specialists provided an alternative system. Usually posing as reporters, CIA men assisted the mutineers in a disinformation campaign to spread phony news about Marcos's intentions.

Marcos could have routed the rebels at the start, when they were weak. Instead he waffled, later claiming that he was being humane. Actually he distrusted his own troops to obey his orders, and he also feared the opprobrium of American opinion. By Sunday afternoon, Manila was delirious. The boulevard between the army camps was a human sea, the crowd surging and receding like a tide as government forces arrived and retreated and returned. Demonstrators carried banners demanding Marcos's resignation. Rebel soldiers, their flag patches inverted, mingled with the throng. One of several climaxes came when loyalist tanks lumbered into the area. As people chanted hymns, priests and nuns knelt in prayer before the machines, and children pressed flowers on the crews. The tanks retired, the people advanced and the tanks withdrew. The tension continued through the day, the crowd cheering each small victory. The Edsa Revolution subsequently became a legend, encapsulated in Cory's escutcheon: People Power.

A surreal electronic battle was also going on as Marcos, Ver, Enrile, Ramos and various intermediaries haggled and bargained over the telephone. Nor was television forgotten. Ramos appeared on *Meet the Press,* vowing to defeat Marcos "by sheer numbers," while Marcos, on the same program, threatened revenge: "We will bide our time, disperse the civilians and then handle Enrile and Ramos." He had been legally elected and would not resign, Marcos insisted—adding, "I don't believe President Reagan would ask me to step down."

Crafting the U.S. Response

Washington is 13 hours behind Manila, and reports from the U.S. embassy were swamping the State Department on Saturday morning. At three o'clock that afternoon, Shultz assembled a few of his staff in his elegant seventh-floor office. They were dressed casually, the weekend custom. Among them were Michael H. Armacost, former U.S. ambassador in Manila and now under secretary of state; Paul D. Wolfowitz, the assistant secretary for Asia; and Charles Hill, Shultz's close aide and alter ego, a diligent professional with a razor-sharp mind. Even at this late stage, they were struggling to shape a firm Philippine policy—proof again that policies are often forged in the heat of crisis rather than in cool contemplation.

Slow, laconic and deliberate, Shultz had watched the problem ripen into a crisis, awaiting the moment to act. Seeing that moment, he said: "Marcos is unraveling. At some point we have to tell him it's over, and offer him asylum in the United States." Armacost observed that the picture was still a blur as assorted Filipino factions jockeyed for position. "Once they see a major swing," Shultz replied, "they'll try to save themselves." Hill pleaded for a quick U.S. decision. "Don't underestimate Marcos," he stressed. "If his opponents don't move fast, he'll bring in forces from the provinces and roll over them. We could see Enrile begging for his life and house arrest, and we'll end up with the Marcos dictatorship versus the Communists." Shultz, agreeing, proposed that a statement be drafted for Reagan, pledging a "safe haven" for Marcos and his family. Even so, Shultz was not sanguine.

Marcos was not "going to bend," he went on—and nothing would embarrass Reagan more than being rebuffed by him. Besides, Shultz added, Reagan "isn't the guy to pull the plug on Marcos." So, the staff concluded, the only approach for the moment was to warn Marcos against using force—as Bosworth was doing in Manila. But the crisis still begged for action, and Shultz decided on a meeting the next morning of the National Security Planning Group, the senior policymaking committee.

The group gathered at nine o'clock around the dining room table of his house in suburban Bethesda as his wife, Helena, served coffee and homemade blueberry muffins. Those present included Weinberger, Armacost, Vice Admiral John M. Poindexter, the president's national security adviser, and Robert M.

Gates, the deputy CIA director, pinch-hitting for Casey. Habib was there, having arrived the night before from Manila. Shultz had just received a message from Bosworth: "Marcos will not draw the conclusion that he must leave unless President Reagan puts it to him directly. Go for a dignified transition out." The problem now was plain, if difficult: how to persuade Reagan to tell Marcos to quit.

Leading off, Habib reported that Marcos was isolated, looked "horrible" and refused "to realize that he faces a widespread movement to dump him." When Shultz cited A. M. Rosenthal's description of Cory as "vacant," Habib dismissed Rosenthal as "a bird of passage [who] flies, perches and then flies away." If Marcos crushed the Enrile mutiny, Habib went on, he would move against Cory next. Shultz concurred: A Marcos police state would polarize the situation and benefit the Communists. He reflected on the damage caused the United States by these "total shifts," like the chaos that followed the falls of Diem and the shah. "We pay a heavy price for our past," he said. Pursuing the point, Weinberger asked, "What happens in the Philippines after Marcos goes?" Habib replied: "It's not Iran. There is a democratic opposition backed by the Catholic Church." When Shultz interposed, "We have a great store of goodwill," Habib pressed on: "If we want to have some control over the situation, we must move fast to a transition." After a brief silence, Shultz declared: "Our conclusion is unanimous. Now we need scenarios."

Shultz's Script

"Forget reconciliation," Habib began. Cory would not deal with Marcos. The group then offered proposals, one by Weinberger for a new election. "Without a new election I have trouble," he said. "You have trouble with everything," Shultz retorted. "A new election is a must," Weinberger insisted. Gates interceded: "Let's be realistic, not legalistic. The public view is that Aquino won. So we have to think of a way to install her in power and give Marcos a fig leaf to depart. Aquino in, Marcos out." Again Weinberger objected, submitting that Reagan would be distressed if he "publicly appeared" to be dumping Marcos.

Poindexter agreed. Someone suggested doing nothing, to which Shultz answered, "There's a lot to be said for that." Habib thundered: "Give Marcos a chance to stay, and he'll hang on. He has to go!" Shultz, alarmed by the danger of bloodshed if Marcos dug in, discursively recalled his experiences as a marine in a bloody battle against the Japanese during World War II. Then, back on track, he recommended public statements aimed at Marcos, coupled with an emissary to him, perhaps Senator Paul Laxalt (R-Nev.) again. He called another session at the State Department after lunch, in case Reagan convened a meeting for that day. As he rose from the table, Habib said, "Don't assume a quick solution."

The same cast met in Shultz's office at two o'clock, now with an acute sense of urgency. It was three o'clock on Monday morning in Manila, and Bosworth reported that Marcos might attack the rebels at daybreak. A decision by Reagan was vital before then. Hill, who had attended the morning session, had taken notes in his spidery handwriting: *Marcos can't govern . . . Force favors left, bad for us . . . We have more options now than later . . . Do right by Marcos, departure in safety and dignity . . . Presidential phone call . . . Broker transition . . . Public call for no force.* Using the notes, Shultz personally wrote a step-by-step script for Reagan, proposing that Laxalt fly to Manila with a presidential message urging Marcos to resign, with Habib accompanying him to broker the transition.

President's Nod

At three o'clock, the group gathered in the White House Situation Room for a formal National Security Council meeting. Vice President George Bush and Treasury Secretary James A. Baker 3rd were there along with Casey, who had missed the discussions until then. As Reagan listened, the session rapidly became a verbal brawl between Regan, his chief of staff, and Habib. Regan, as one participant recalled, "didn't understand or care to understand" the issue, but "thought that he was conveying Reagan's thoughts." Evoking the Iran analogy, he vehemently opposed scuttling Marcos, called Cory an unknown quantity and warned against "opening the door to communism." Habib, after repeating his case, concluded, "The Marcos era has ended." Endorsing Habib's assessment, Shultz said: "Nobody believes that Marcos can remain in power. He's had it." As the debate droned on, Reagan's attention waned—except when new reports arrived of imminent violence in Manila. He appeared to the anti-Marcos faction to be turning around when, at one point, he remarked that Marcos had to be "approached carefully" and "asked rather than told" to depart. He declined to telephone Marcos and tell him to go, nor would he send him a personal message. Nor would he countenance a replay of Jimmy Carter's refusal to allow the shah to enter the United States until he was near death. Marcos, he affirmed, could have asylum in America. So, as the 90-minute meeting closed, Reagan had acquiesced to deposing his "old friend."

Two potential catastrophes haunted Reagan and his staff. One was the danger that Marcos, in a final desperate attempt to prevail, might attack the rebel camps, slaughtering masses of civilians—on world television. Equally horrible was the possibility that the mutineers might capture and murder Marcos and his family, thus reenacting the assassination of Diem in the South Vietnamese coup encouraged by the United States. To avert either disaster, Reagan approved a public statement warning Marcos that he "would cause untold damage to the relationship between our two governments" if he used force, and threatened to suspend his military aid unless he obeyed. But Reagan's decision to tell Marcos to leave was kept secret for the moment in the hope that, through private persuasion, he might go voluntarily and thus be spared the embarrassment of having been removed under U.S. pressure.

Three channels were operating. Nancy, constantly being telephoned by Imelda, told her that she and Ferdinand would "certainly" be welcomed in America. Marcos's labor minister, Blas F. Ople, had come to Washington to lobby for him, and Shultz advised him to urge his boss to depart gracefully. Shultz also called Bosworth, reaching him at about six o'clock on Monday morning, Manila time. He ordered him to inform

Marcos that his "time was up," and that "we will make the transition as peaceful as possible." Marcos angrily rejected Bosworth and, going on television, claimed to be in control. "I will fight to the last breath," he intoned, "even though my family cowers in terror in the palace."

Reagan afterward said with admiration that Marcos "did not want bloodshed or civil strife" and had shown restraint as a result. In reality, Marcos knew as his troops defected in droves to the rebels that a military response was too late. He tried to bargain. Calling Enrile, he proposed a coalition excluding Cory. Enrile, wary of Marcos's wiles, refused and urged Cory to legitimize herself quickly in an inauguration—and she did the next day. Equally obsessed with legitimacy, Marcos set his own inauguration for the following day. On Monday afternoon in Washington, while still pursuing the private conduits, Reagan approved a public plea to Marcos to quit: "Attempts to prolong the life of the present regime by violence are futile. A solution to this crisis can only be achieved through a peaceful transition to a new government." Marcos received the message at three o'clock in the morning, Tuesday, February 25, Manila time, and immediately called Laxalt in Washington, hoping through him to reach Reagan.

There, on Monday afternoon, Shultz, Habib and Armacost were in the Capitol building, secretly briefing 30 key members of Congress, including Laxalt. The telephone call from Marcos to Laxalt interrupted the session. Marcos wanted the word straight from Reagan: Was the statement about a "transition" real or another State Department plot? With Shultz, Habib and Armacost hovering over him, Laxalt confirmed it. The conversation lasted 20 minutes, Marcos's raspy voice betraying his exhaustion. He essayed alternatives, like a "power-sharing" deal with Cory. After all, he said, he was a veteran at fighting Communists and negotiating with foreign creditors. Floating another idea, he might serve as Cory's "senior adviser" while remaining president until the end of his original term in 1987. Laxalt promised to consult Reagan and call him back.

The briefing finished, Laxalt accompanied Shultz to the State

Department to drop off Habib and Armacost. As they drove through a snow flurry, Laxalt asked whether Marcos's proposals for a "power-sharing" or "advisory" deal might work. Armacost, recoiling from the ingenuous question, explained that Marcos would eventually rally his loyalists and "you would have civil war." Laxalt then went with Shultz to the White House to confer with Reagan, Poindexter and Regan in the Oval Office. The meeting lasted 13 minutes. Laxalt recounted his talk with Marcos, and again raised the proposal for an accommodation with Cory. "Impractical," said Shultz. Reagan, nodding assent, added that Marcos would be welcome in the United States "if he saw fit."

Exit Marcos

Laxalt moved to Poindexter's office and, fulfilling his promise, telephoned Marcos—who at five o'clock in the morning in Manila awaited the call. With Shultz guiding him, Laxalt told Marcos that Reagan had vetoed a deal with Cory but offered him asylum in America. Marcos, still angling for the Olympian word, asked if Reagan wanted him to resign. Laxalt ducked the question. "Senator," Marcos pressed, "what do you think? Should I step down?" Laxalt responded without hesitation: "I think you should cut and cut cleanly. I think the time has come." There was a silence so long that Laxalt, wondering whether they had been disconnected, asked, "Mr. President, are you there?" "Yes," responded Marcos in a thin voice. "I am so very, very disappointed."

Bosworth, who had been planning Marcos's departure for two days, decided on the advice of his military aides that a helicopter lift would be safest. He arranged to take the Marcoses from the Malacañang across the Pasig River by barge, then fly them to Clark field and from there to the United States. The project, ready on Tuesday morning, was soon delayed. Marcos wanted to hold his inauguration ritual. There was packing, dawdling, telephoning friends, attempts at last-ditch deals. Finally, in the late afternoon, the Marcos family and its retinue of 60 were braced to depart. Show biz to the end, Marcos and Imelda stepped out onto a palace balcony, peered at a crowd of supporters and hecklers, and sang a farewell duet: "Because of You."

The helicopters flew the Marcoses to Clark field, where they were to board a U.S. Air Force transport for the United States. But Marcos balked, asking instead to spend "a couple of days" with his family and friends in Ilocos Norte, his home province. His escort, Major General Theodore Allen, the chief American military-aid adviser in the Philippines, telephoned Bosworth, who called Washington, which suggested that he contact Cory. She was torn between her gratitude to Marcos for releasing Ninoy to have heart surgery and her fear that he might stir his native region to revolt. After consulting her advisers, who favored a quick exit, she asked Bosworth: "Is he really ill?" "Aside from being exhausted, I don't know," Bosworth replied. "Well," she said, "let him stay the night at Clark and after that he must leave the country." Soon afterward, the Clark commander reported to Bosworth that loyalist Marcos troops were nearing the base, saying, "I want that guy out of here now." Bosworth agreed. Allen told Marcos, "You can go anywhere you want as long as it's out of the country." That night, the Marcoses and their children took off for Guam, their ultimate destination Hawaii. Once aloft, Imelda began to sing "New York, New York."

Administration Victory, Marcos Indictment

The Reagan Administration reveled in the neat, bloodless change, as did even its fiercest press critics. "It is a long time since Americans of all political views have felt so good about a transforming event abroad," wrote Anthony Lewis, the liberal *New York Times* columnist, extolling Reagan's "great skill and impeccable timing." Morton I. Abramowitz, one of the senior State Department officials who had labored to remove Marcos, termed the conjuncture of events "luck, sheer luck."

Reagan never forgave Cory for denying Marcos a visit to his native region, but his faith in Marcos sank as the proof of plunder emerged. The loot found in the Malacañang was shocking enough. Worse yet was the evidence of racketeering by Marcos during his rule and even after his exile in Hawaii. Nearly 100

President
and Mrs. Marcos
hold their own
"inaugural" hours
before being flown
to exile in
Hawaii.

Tucci—Gamma/Liaison

civil suits were filed against him in the Philippines, seeking a total of almost $100 billion. Meanwhile, a grand jury in Honolulu began to probe his attempts to buy weapons to stage a comeback, a breach of the Neutrality Act, and another in Pittsburgh, Pennsylvania, started to look into alleged kickbacks in the Westinghouse nuclear project. Marcos refused to face a panel in Alexandria, Virginia, which formally charged one of General Ver's cronies with fraud in connection with official arms purchases. The big sensation, however, was the indictment on October 21, 1988, by a New York grand jury. The Marcoses and eight others, including the Saudi Arabian fixer Adnan M. Khashoggi, were accused of embezzling more than $100 million from the Philippine government to acquire three Manhattan buildings, defrauding American banks to finance the deal. The investigation also revealed 20 secret Marcos accounts in a Swiss bank and other clandestine deposits elsewhere. With Marcos too sick to travel, Imelda appeared in court to post $5 million bail, lent by one of her few remaining chums—the aged tobacco heiress Doris Duke. Bush was then campaigning for President, and for Reagan to defend the Marcoses would have tarnished the Republican ticket. Nor could Reagan afford to alienate Cory, who had just signed an interim bases agreement with the United States. Reagan did nothing—though he was "pained," a senior Administration official confided to me, by the final degradation of his old friend.

5

Democracy Restored:
Cory Aquino Victorious

The miracle of Cory's victory inspired in Filipinos—and in many of her American admirers—the dream that she would now perform economic, social and political miracles. The end of tyranny and the revival of democracy euphorically signaled a new era of peace and prosperity. As Cory began to pick up the pieces of her shattered country, however, she faced an array of staggering problems that no individual, even with divine guidance, could resolve rapidly. Nor was she inclined to promote drastic measures. Though she labeled her overthrow of Marcos a revolution, it was really a restoration.

Cory was not a revolutionary determined to renovate the society from top to bottom. Essentially conservative, as befits a member of her class, she sought to resurrect the institutions dismantled by Marcos rather than construct a new system. In the process, she revived the old dynasties he had dispossessed, including her own family, and they jockeyed to regain their former positions of privilege. She also lacked experience and confidence in her ability to govern, and at first surrounded herself with a cacophony of advisers, each tugging in different directions. Prudent and uncertain, she was reluctant to take advantage of her immense popularity to impose her leadership, preferring instead to rule by moral example. She gradually began to assert herself and showed in certain instances that she had the right stuff, but she squandered her initial momentum, thereby losing a unique opportunity to introduce reforms. Into the vacuum poured a multiplicity of undisciplined, selfish, querulous factions eager to advance their own ambitions. There appeared to be little prospect for the profound and pervasive changes vital to deter the spread of the Communist insurgency or perhaps even the return of a Marcos in different guise.

Particularly dramatic were the skepticism, disappointment and apprehension of the groups that had catapulted Cory to power: the intellectuals, businessmen, clergy and army. They clamored for stability, yet they carped at her incessantly, their behavior seeming to mirror two antithetical ingredients in the Philippine heritage: an Asian reverence for authority and a Latin penchant for hypercriticism. The uncomfortable mixture did not make Cory's task any easier as she wrestled with a job she had never wanted, and she responded to their taunts by saying, "What is your alternative?"

Coups, Courage and a New Constitution

A foremost Filipino writer, F. Sionil José, originally an ardent supporter, unleashed a tirade in the summer of 1987, faulting her for failing to "translate her massive popularity into action," warning that "unless she changes quickly she will bring this country to ruin." Jaime Ongpin, her able finance secretary, who had rallied the business community to her side, committed suicide in despair after a series of squabbles inside her cabinet. Father Joaquin Bernas, a Jesuit scholar and one of her closest campaign advisers, vented his frustration publicly. Her "revolution" had been "perfect," he said in an interview—"a 360-degree turn back to where we were before . . . still no social justice, still corruption and economic deprivation." "The people," he added, "are not getting the president they voted for." Doronila, editor of *The*

Manila Chronicle, echoed the same theme: "There has been no national agenda, no initiatives. Cory is a passive president who follows, not leads." The army manifested its dissatisfaction in five coup attempts during her first year and a half in office—the most serious of them staged in August 1986 by Colonel Honasan, who had led the mutiny against Marcos. The surprise revolt nearly succeeded. "Until it was over," a Pentagon official remarked later, "we didn't realize how dicey the situation was." Cory showed unique courage and serenity during the coup, in which her son was injured. "I am fatalistic," she again told me afterward, candidly admitting her belief in predestination.

Most of the criticism of her was centered in Manila, a city that flourishes on political gossip. Out in the rural areas, her capacity for survival gave her an aura of sanctity that reinforced her popular appeal. Early in 1987, she held a referendum to approve her new constitution, a thick, turgid document that defied easy comprehension. It won overwhelming endorsement—actually overwhelming endorsement for Cory. Her legislative elections in May 1987 and local contests a year later both drew big turnouts, even though she had declined to create a political party. Still the malaise continued.

Cory Tries to Forge Unity

Striving to reconcile the disparate elements that had backed her crusade, Cory at first cobbled together a coalition cabinet. It was a basket of crabs. She chose as her chief of staff a leftist lawyer improbably named Joker Arroyo, to whom she was grateful for his defense of Ninoy. A schemer who bore an uncanny resemblance to the young Bonaparte, he was anathema to the army for his past battles over human rights violations, while his administrative incompetence appalled technocrats like Ongpin. Enrile, her defense secretary, was meanwhile plotting against her, and Laurel, the vice-president who doubled as foreign secretary, had his own priorities in mind. She dumped Enrile and later fired Arroyo and Ongpin, and Laurel subsequently quit the cabinet to remain, incongruously, vice-president in opposition. Cory was hailed for firmness, but two precious years had been wasted.

She blundered, her critics claimed, by refusing to decree agrarian reforms under her revolutionary powers, and instead passed the buck to the new legislature. Her virtuous purpose was to respect democratic procedure. Predictably, the debate over reforms dragged on until June 1988, when representatives of the landed interests finally voted a law riddled with loopholes. Enforcement was delegated to local councils usually controlled by landowners, who in addition won the right to challenge decisions in court—an endless process. One of the clauses, evidently sponsored by Cory's brother, José Cojuangco, would exempt their family sugar plantation by instituting a "profit-sharing" arrangement for the workers—with the proprietors determining the profit. Cory's own secretary of agriculture, Carlos "Sonny" Domínguez, who had drafted a comprehensive plan, was dismayed. "More than anything," he said, "we needed radical land reform, but Cory was too cautious. She had an opportunity and she blew it."

A curious trace of nostalgia for authority emerged in observers like *The Manila Chronicle* editor Doronila, who spent the Marcos years in exile in Australia. He saw in the legislature a "circus of atomized members, each acting on behalf of individual or at best limited interests" to block reforms. The "impasse," he wrote, might tempt Cory to become another Marcos or perhaps spur a military junta "to seize power in the name of national development."

But agrarian reform of any kind faced an immense obstacle: money. Aside from paying landowners for their property, the program had to furnish farmers with credit, seeds, tools and, above all, training. One estimate put the cost at more than $7 billion for a 10-year period, a sum the Philippines could not even begin to contemplate, given the crippled economy Cory inherited in the aftermath of Marcos's egregious profligacy. Attempts to raise funds from the sale of government companies had bogged down, and the prospects for foreign aid looked bleak.

Cory rosily declared in July 1988 that she had overcome the Marcos legacy, and that "the economy has taken off." A growth rate of about 6 percent in the gross national product for the previous year seemed to prove her point. So too did the appearance of Manila during my visits. I saw new houses going up in residential suburbs and a booming stock exchange. Restaurants, nightclubs and discos were packed, and shopping centers were thronged with buyers of furniture, refrigerators, air conditioners and other big-tag items. The picture was both true and false. The urban middle classes were thriving, due in part to higher salaries for government employees, but the prosperity touched neither the sprawling city slums nor the countryside. A confidential World Bank study completed in the summer of 1988 observed that "there are more poor people in the Philippines today than at any time in recent history," adding that their plight "has worsened during the past three decades." Of the population of 56 million Filipinos, the report said, more than half lived in "absolute poverty"—meaning that their income "did not enable them to satisfy basic needs." The survey repeated a familiar litany: the government's neglect of rural areas, widespread tax evasion by the rich, a grossly inequitable land-ownership pattern. Even with an unusually high growth rate of 6 percent, the study concluded, the Philippines would return to its 1982 economic level only by 1992—and at that barring a crisis in the world market for sugar, copra and other commodities.

Debt and Corruption

A major impediment to economic growth was servicing the foreign debt of nearly $28 billion contracted by Marcos, which drained the country of 40 percent of its earnings from exports. Another plague was corruption, which in 1988 cost the Philippine treasury $2.5 billion, or about one third of the national budget. As Cardinal Sin quipped, "Ali Baba Marcos fled, leaving behind the 40 thieves." It differed from Marcos's plundering, a state enterprise directed from his palace. Nobody could fault Cory for personal dishonesty, but despite her campaign promise to promote integrity, she was confronted by an endemic problem.

Returning to Manila during her years in office, I again listened to the same old tales of corruption: customs agents engaged in smuggling, kickbacks on government contracts, fake licenses, payoffs to cops. A commission created by Cory to recover Marcos's "ill-gotten gains" was revamped after the revelation that its members had stolen some of those gains. One of Cory's early backers, newspaper publisher Joaquín Roces, whom Marcos had jailed, startled her at a public meeting by saying that her regime was guilty of "self-aggrandizement and service to vested interests, relatives and friends." He was transparently referring to her brother José, known as "Peping," and his wife, Margarita, or "Tingting," the reputed bosses of enterprises ranging from a gambling monopoly to the illicit barter trade in the south. A brother-in-law, Ricardo "Baby" Lopa, was denounced by the Manila press for having acquired for a pittance the companies that Imelda's brother "Kokoy" had acquired for a pittance. The petty graft by minor bureaucrats reflected their struggle to survive amid dire poverty. The reluctance to pursue offenders mirrored age-old kinship loyalties. Cory told a reporter that she had warned members of her family against abusing their position. "Short of ordering them to hibernate or go into exile," she said, "I don't know what else I can do."

The economy has also been stunted by the spiraling population, which is bound to intensify into an unmanageable problem in the years ahead. But the Catholic hierarchy has denounced birth control as "dehumanizing and immoral," and Cory has evaded the issue out of religious piety. When I first visited the Philippines in the late 1950s, there were about 25 million Filipinos. The population has doubled since then and is expected to double again by the year 2010, and the implications of that projection are horrendous. To keep pace with the explosion, according to a study in the *Far Eastern Economic Review,* the Philippines will have to increase food production by 40 percent by the end of the century, in addition to providing for thousands of schools and clinics and millions of jobs. "The pressure of people on land," a World Bank report declared in 1988, "has brought about the impoverishment of a large part of the rural sector." It has been that impoverishment, probably more than any other single factor, that has fueled the spread of the Communist insurgency—a war that plainly cannot be won by battalions and bullets.

Combating the Communist Insurgency

Cory announced in July 1988 that "this may be remembered as the year the insurgency was broken." But her optimistic forecast was soon punctured by a leak to a Manila newspaper of a secret military study stating that the rebels had gained "the tactical initiative in major engagements." As usual, the truth was somewhere in between. The Communists made a grave error by boycotting the election that lifted Cory to power. Their chief spokesman, Satur Ocampo, candidly admitted the mistake to me, saying, "We failed to benefit from the popular sentiment against Marcos." The movement was further weakened by disputes between advocates of a political approach and champions of armed struggle. In many places, local revolts against the government were proliferating, eluding the control of the Communists. Still, the New People's Army, as the Communist guerrillas called their force, remained dynamic, organized and menacing. By contrast, the Philippine military establishment continued to be nagged by shortages of supplies, command rivalries and other difficulties—though its morale had risen since the Marcos era. Honasan's abortive coup ironically helped by alerting Cory to the need to raise the wages of soldiers and improve their conditions.

An effective check to the Communists has been a variety of vigilante groups, like one in the Mindanao capital of Davao known as Alsa Masa or "Up with the Masses." Its commander, Lieutenant Colonel Franco M. Calida, advertised himself to the press from an office decorated with a big poster of Sylvester Stallone as Rambo. In 1986, when I visited Davao, the Communists controlled a slum district called Agdao. Calida cleaned out the area within two years with his 3,000 men, numbers of them Communist defectors. But his and other groups, acting without official supervision, summarily killed suspects and settled old feuds. Some, like the Tadtad, which means "chop," were mystical, cannibalistic cults that beheaded victims and ate their livers. Cory originally applauded the vigilantes as prototypes of "people power," but their abuses tarnished her name with human rights activists. The Lawyers Committee for International Human Rights, a New York-based organization, concluded in June

1988 after months of research that "the human rights of Filipinos have suffered grave violations on a wide scale." Criticism from such organizations, which had pleaded for Ninoy during his imprisonment, grated a raw nerve in Cory, and she angrily refuted the charge. The director of her human rights commission indirectly confirmed the complaint, however, saying that "in an environment of war . . . it is most difficult, if not impossible, to prevent brutality.

The Future of a 'Special Relationship'

The question posed repeatedly since Cory was catapulted into office is: "Can she make it?"

Bosworth, writing in *The Washington Post* late in 1987, had a judicious reply. "The question itself requires definition. If 'making it' means turning the Philippines into a stable, prosperous, self-confident model of democracy in a developing country, the answer is clearly no. The problems are too difficult, the Filipino sense of nationhood too weak and the time given to Aquino until the end of her term in 1992 too short. On the other hand, if the question is whether her government can survive and she can continue to make gradual but important progress, then my answer is yes." Whatever happened, Bosworth emphasized, the future of the Philippines hinged on the Filipinos themselves.

But not without the Americans.

In the aftermath of Marcos's downfall, the Filipinos faced obstacles that they could not conceivably hurdle alone. Their economy was burdened by a foreign debt that had put them at the mercy of their foreign creditors. They needed foreign investment and foreign aid. Only the United States could carry them through the crisis—and, even then, the going would be precarious.

Yet a vocal faction of Manila politicians, journalists, professors and others, determined to assert their nationalism, championed a tougher stance toward the Americans out of a complexity of motives. Some contended that the United States was not being generous enough toward one of its oldest allies while others advocated a clean break with the Americans as an affirmation of Philippine sovereignty. In large measure, the ferment was stimulated by the permissiveness of Cory Aquino's administration. Unshackled from the fetters of the Marcos autocracy, Filipinos were indulging themselves in a feast of freedom. To denounce the United States had always been one of their favorite sports, but they realized that it was a tricky game. And, in the end, they displayed caution.

A turning point came in October 1988, with the agreement signed in Washington to ensure the operation of the U.S. bases in the Philippines until 1991, when a longer-term pact would have to be concluded. Both sides had postured during the bargaining. Cory's foreign secretary, Manglapus, called America's presence in the archipelago a violation of national independence, claiming that the moment had arrived to end the residual colonial relationship. Secretary of State Shultz and other senior U.S. officials threatened to transfer the bases elsewhere, and bolstered their warning by disclosing that the cost of moving would be less than at first anticipated.

Aerial view of Subic Naval Base—one of the two largest U.S. overseas military installations. The United States will continue to operate the base until at least 1991, when the current lease expires.

U.S. Navy Photograph/PHC Lawrence Foster

Money, not principles, ultimately concluded the dispute. After seven months of negotiations, the Filipinos settled for an American aid package of $481 million a year in exchange for the bases—one third of Manglapus's original demand. The deal sparked an outburst from Filipino nationalists, who contended that, once again, U.S. pressure had prevailed.

The compromise was a prelude to fresh discussions to prolong the life of the bases beyond 1991. But the interim accord represented an indirect admission by Filipinos that they desperately needed American assistance—and would for years ahead. Also implicit in the agreement was an understanding on the part of both Americans and Filipinos that, however lopsided, thorny and at times frustrating their "special relationship" might be, it reflected a century of shared experience. Dewey, Taft, MacArthur, Lansdale and Reagan, Aguinaldo, Quezon, Magsaysay, the Marcoses and the Aquinos had marched together through history along with millions of other Americans and Filipinos, and their common past had ordained both their present and their future.

Talking It Over

A Note for Students and Discussion Groups

This issue of the HEADLINE SERIES, like its predecessors, is published for every serious reader, specialized or not, who takes an interest in the subject. Many of our readers will be in classrooms, seminars or community discussion groups. Particularly with them in mind, we present below some discussion questions—suggested as a starting point only—and references for further reading.

Discussion Questions

What effects did Spanish colonialism have on the Philippines? In what ways was it beneficial? In what ways was it detrimental?

How would you characterize the legacy of American colonialism?

Are the Philippines' social and cultural traditions compatible with its development as a democracy?

Do you think, as some Filipinos believe, that the continued presence of the U.S. bases will harm long-term U.S.-Philippine relations? In what ways, if any, are the bases an asset to the Philippines?

More than half of the Filipino population lives in absolute poverty. The number is growing and their plight is worsening. How can the Philippines combat such poverty? What steps might Aquino take to accomplish this? What are the obstacles?

A growing issue for the Philippines is its soaring birthrate which threatens to negate any economic gains. Aquino's government has abandoned support for family planning, and there is a fierce debate between those who favor limiting the population and the Catholic Church which opposes artificial birth control. How do you think Aquino should handle this issue?

What was the aim of the U.S. policy toward the Philippines under Marcos? How would you describe America's role in the Philippine election? Was the U.S. policy successful?

READING LIST

Agoncillo, Teodoro, *A Short History of the Philippines.* New York, New American Library, 1975.

Aquino, Benigno, Jr., "What's Wrong with the Philippines?" *Foreign Affairs,* July 1968. A critique by Ferdinand Marcos's chief political opponent and late husband of Cory Aquino.

Clad, James, "Philippines Population: Go Forth and Multiply." *Far Eastern Economic Review,* October 20, 1988. A survey of the Philippines' soaring birthrate, its destructive effect on economic growth and the debate on birth control.

————, "U.S. Bases in the Philippines: Is the Circus Ending?" *Far Eastern Economic Review,* April 21, 1988. A collection of articles that portray the differing and often clashing views on the U.S. military presence in the Philippines.

Fallow, James, "A Damaged Culture." *The Atlantic Monthly,* January 1987. A provocative essay.

Friend, Theodore, "Marcos and the Philippines." *Orbis,* Fall 1988. U.S. policy toward a regime it was critical of morally but considered strategically important.

Hahn, Emily, *The Islands: America's Imperialist Adventures in the Philippines.* New York, Coward, McCann and Geoghegan, 1981. A useful primer.

Lambertson, David F., "Recent Developments in the Philippines." *Department of State Bulletin,* March 1988. An optimistic overview of the progress made by the Aquino government.

Lande, Carl, ed., *Rebuilding a Nation.* Washington D.C., Washington Institute Press, 1987. In the chapter on President Aquino, author Guy Parker canonizes Cory.

O'Brien, Niall, *Revolution from the Heart: The Extraordinary Record of a Priest's Life and Work Among the Poor of the Philippine Sugarlands.* New York, Oxford University Press, 1987. Elucidates the economic and social problems of the sugar industry.

"Philippines." *Background Notes.* Washington D.C., U.S. Department of State, Bureau of Public Affairs, August 1986.

Pye, Lucian, *Asian Power and Politics.* Cambridge, Mass., Harvard University Press, 1985. An excellent analysis of the impact of social values on politics.

"A Question of Faith." *The Economist* (London), May 7, 1988. A thorough survey of the Philippines under Cory Aquino.

Shaplen, Robert, "The Thin Edge." *The New Yorker,* September 21 and September 28, 1987. A balanced if not very rosy assessment of the Aquino administration.

Steinberg, David Joel, *The Philippines: A Singular and Plural Place.* Boulder, Colo., Westview Press, 1982. A brief but eloquent introduction to the Philippines.

Foreign Policy Association

Since 1918, the Foreign Policy Association's purpose has been to help Americans gain a better understanding of significant issues in U.S. foreign policy and stimulate constructive and informed citizen participation in world affairs.

FPA is independent, nonpartisan and nongovernmental. It is a national, not-for-profit, educational organization whose major function is to define and call wide public attention to those major issues of contemporary foreign policy which government and people must resolve in democratic partnership.

Americans from all walks of life take part in FPA-sponsored meetings with national and world leaders, and in study and discussion programs based on FPA publications. The annual Great Decisions program, based on the briefing book prepared by FPA's editors, involves more than 250,000 Americans in study and discussion of eight of the most important foreign policy issues facing the United States. The year-round HEADLINE SERIES books and special publications bring lively, authoritative resources on current world topics to the general public, to educators and other professionals, and to students in high schools, colleges and universities. And the wider debate and comment FPA's publications stimulate through TV, radio and the print media reach out to more Americans than any other world affairs educational service in the nation.